ALL-TIME KEYBOARD FAVOURITES

WISE PUBLICATIONS
PART OF THE MUSIC SALES GROUP
LONDON / NEW YORK / PARIS / SYDNEY / COPENHAGEN / BERLIN / MADRID / TOKYO

Published by
Wise Publications
14-15 Berners Street,
London W1T 3LJ, UK.

Exclusive Distributors:
Music Sales Limited
Distribution Centre, Newmarket Road,
Bury St Edmunds, Suffolk IP33 3YB, UK.
Music Sales Corporation
257 Park Avenue South,
New York, NY 10010, USA.
Music Sales Pty Limited
20 Resolution Drive, Caringbah,
NSW 2229, Australia.

Order No. AM995995
ISBN 978-1-84772-834-0

Edited by Jenni Wheeler.
Cover design by Ruth Keating.

Printed in the EU.

Your Guarantee of Quality
As publishers, we strive to produce every book to the
highest commercial standards.
This book has been carefully designed to minimise awkward
page turns and to make playing from it a real pleasure.
Particular care has been given to specifying acid-free, neutral-sized paper
made from pulps which have not been elemental chlorine bleached.
This pulp is from farmed sustainable forests and was
produced with special regard for the environment.
Throughout, the printing and binding have been planned to
ensure a sturdy, attractive publication which should give years of enjoyment.
If your copy fails to meet our high standards,
please inform us and we will gladly replace it.

www.musicsales.com

Ain't No Sunshine

Words & Music by Bill Withers

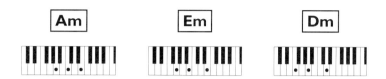

Voice: **Acoustic Guitar**
Rhythm: **Ballad**
Tempo: ♩ = 80

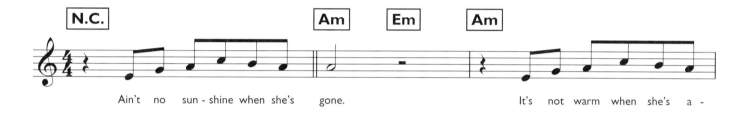

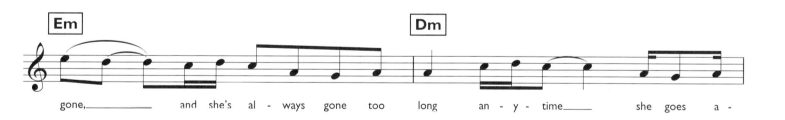

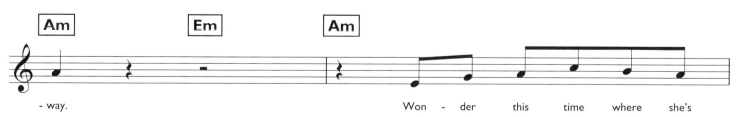

gone,   won - der if she's gone to   stay.

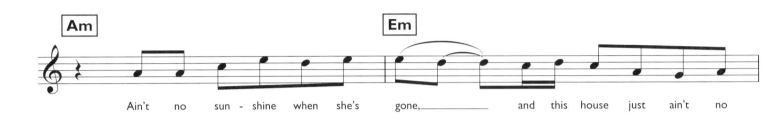
Ain't no sun - shine when she's   gone,_____ and this house just ain't no

home   an - y - time_____   she goes   a - way.

And I know, I know, I know,__ I know, I know, I know, I know,__ I know,__ I know I

know, I know,__ I know,__ I know, I know, I know I know, I know, I know, I know,__ I know,

I know, I know, I know,__ I know, I know, I know. Hey, I ought to leave the young thing a -

lone,____ but ain't no sun - shine when she's gone.____

____ Ain't no sun - shine when she's gone,

on - ly dark - ness ev - 'ry day.

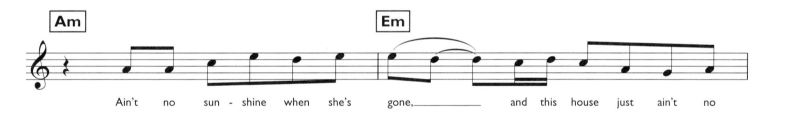

Ain't no sun - shine when she's gone,____ and this house just ain't no

home an - y - time____ she goes a - way,

an - y - time____ she goes a - way.

The Air That I Breathe

Words & Music by Albert Hammond & Mike Hazelwood

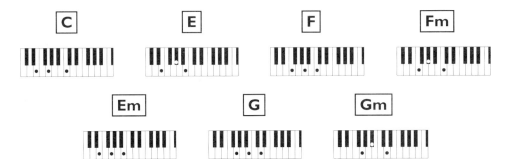

Voice: **Electric Guitar**
Rhythm: **Rock Ballad**
Tempo: ♩ = 88

If I could make a wish___ I think I'd pass,___

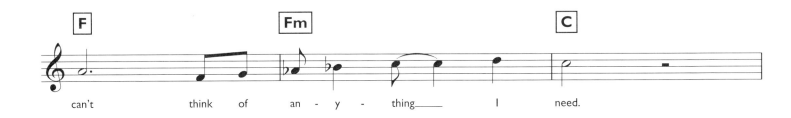

can't think of an - y - thing___ I need.

No cig - a - rettes, no sleep,___ no light, no sound,

___ noth - ing to eat no books___ to read.

Mak - - ing love with you_____ has left me

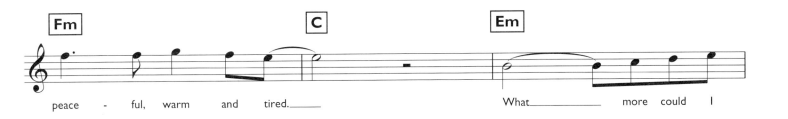

peace - ful, warm and tired.____ What_____ more could I

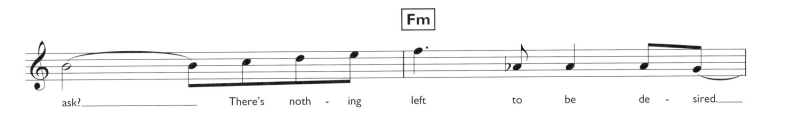

ask?_____ There's noth - ing left to be de - sired.____

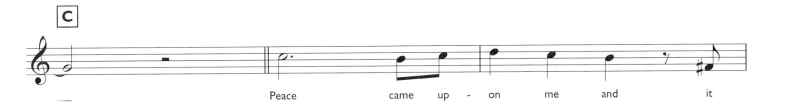

____ Peace came up - on me and it

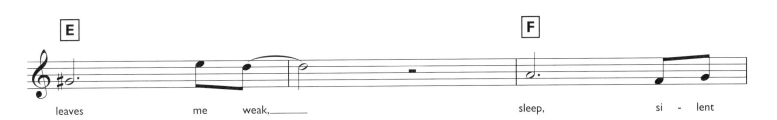

leaves me weak,____ sleep, si - lent

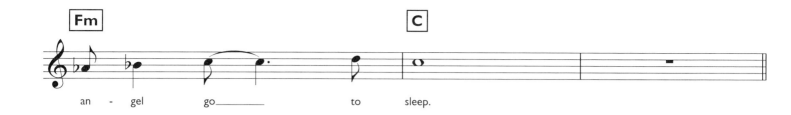

an - gel go_____ to sleep.

Some - times,____ all I need is the air_____ that I breathe__ and to

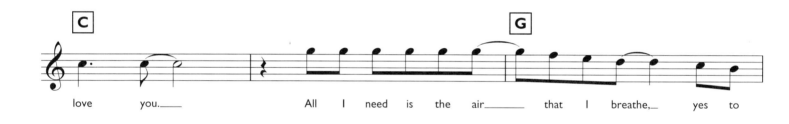

love you.____ All I need is the air_____ that I breathe,__ yes to

love you.____ All I need is the air_____ that I breathe._

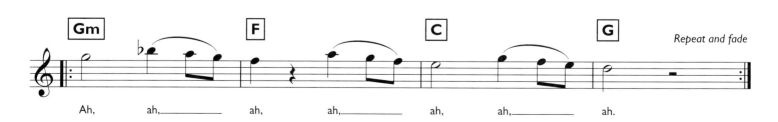

Repeat and fade

Ah, ah,_____ ah, ah,_____ ah, ah,_____ ah.

Baker Street

Words & Music by Gerry Rafferty

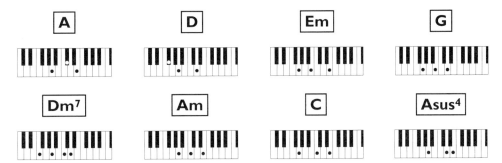

Voice: **Piano**

Rhythm: **Pop Ballad**

Tempo: ♩ = 120

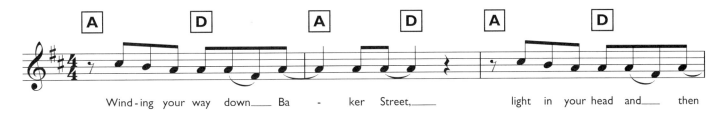

Wind-ing your way down Ba - ker Street, light in your head and then

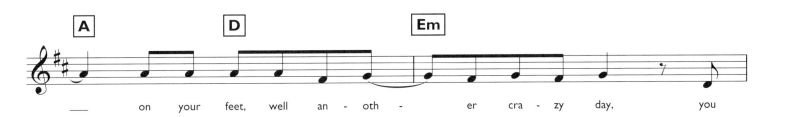

on your feet, well an - oth - er cra - zy day, you

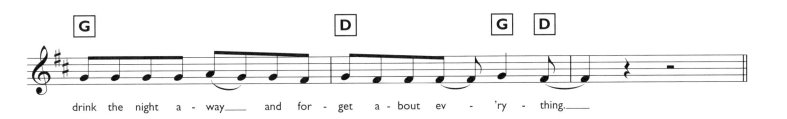

drink the night a - way and for - get a - bout ev - 'ry - thing.

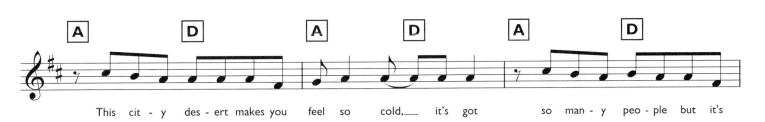

This cit - y des - ert makes you feel so cold, it's got so man - y peo - ple but it's

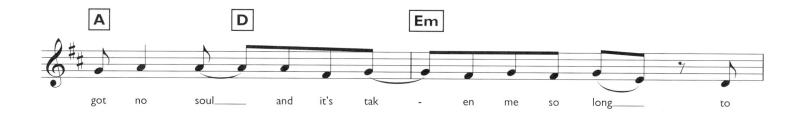

got no soul___ and it's tak - en me so long___ to

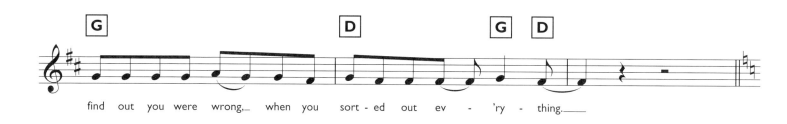

find out you were wrong,___ when you sort - ed out ev - 'ry - thing.___

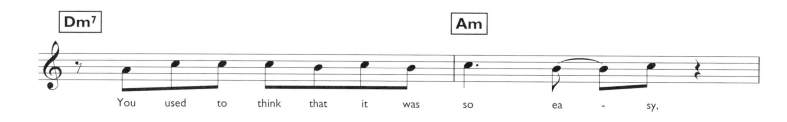

You used to think that it was so ea - sy,

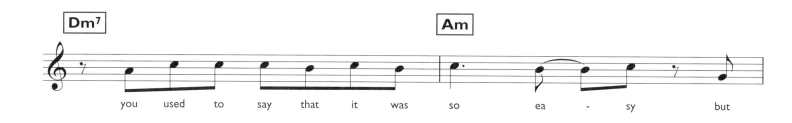

you used to say that it was so ea - sy but

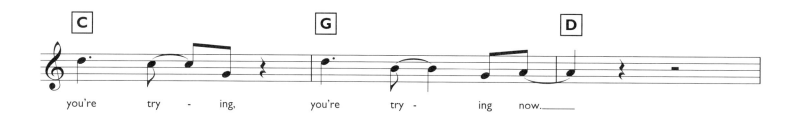

you're try - ing, you're try - ing now.___

An - oth - er year and then you'll be hap - py,

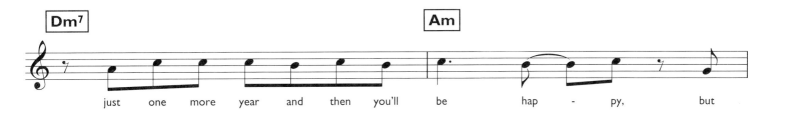

just one more year and then you'll be hap - py, but

you're cry - ing, you're cry - ing now.____

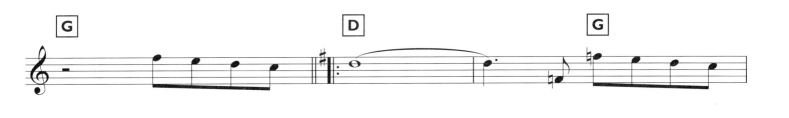

Repeat and fade

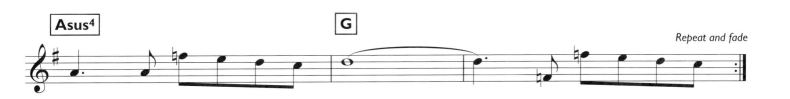

Brown Eyed Girl

Words & Music by Van Morrison

Voice: **Soprano Sax**
Rhythm: **Soft Rock**
Tempo: ♩ = 130

Hey, where did we go, days__ when the rains__ came?

Down__ in the hol - low, play - ing a new__ game.

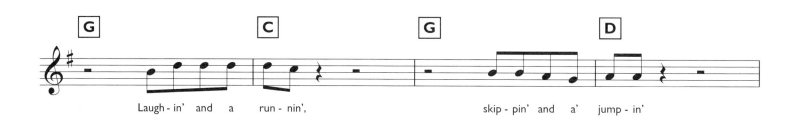

Laugh - in' and a run - nin', skip - pin' and a' jump - in'

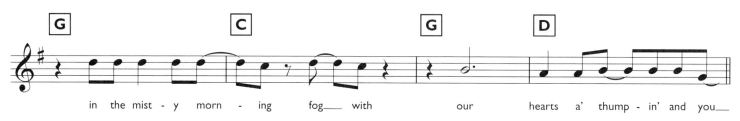

in the mist - y morn - ing fog__ with our hearts a' thump - in' and you__

my brown eyed girl,

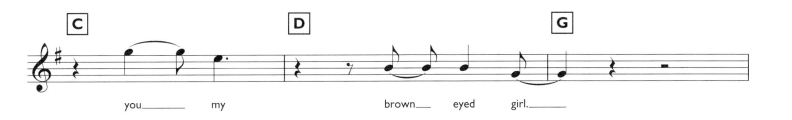

you my brown eyed girl.

Do you re - mem - ber when we used to sing?

Sha - la - la - la - la - la - la - la - la - la - la - la - la.

Repeat and fade

Sha - la - la - la - la - la - la - la - la - la - la - la - la.

Can't Take My Eyes Off You

Words & Music by Bob Crewe & Bob Gaudio

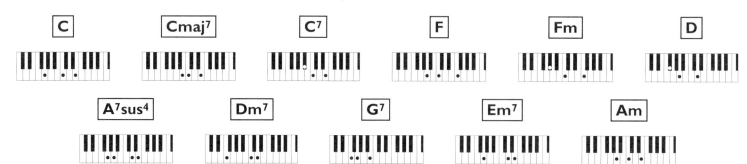

Voice: **Acoustic Guitar**
Rhythm: **Pop Ballad**
Tempo: ♩ = 120

You're just too good to be true,_____ can't take my eyes off of you,_____ you'd be like

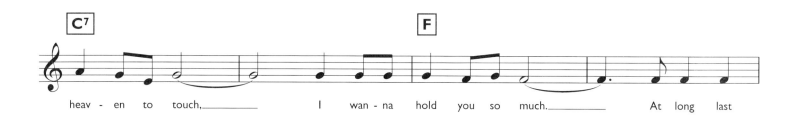

heav - en to touch,_____ I wan - na hold you so much._____ At long last

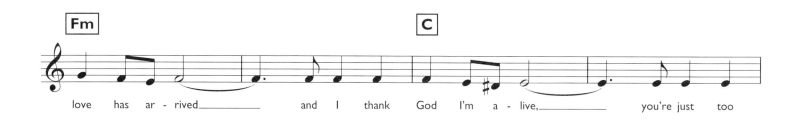

love has ar - rived_____ and I thank God I'm a - live,_____ you're just too

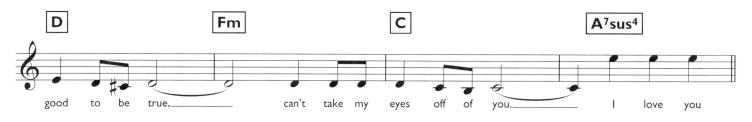

good to be true,_____ can't take my eyes off of you. I love you

ba - by___ and if it's quite al - right,___ I need you ba - by,___ to warm the

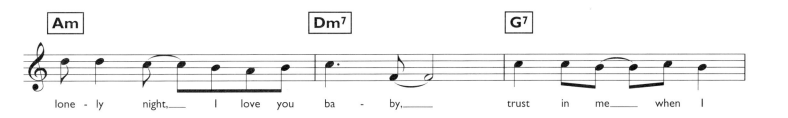

lone - ly night,___ I love you ba - by,___ trust in me___ when I

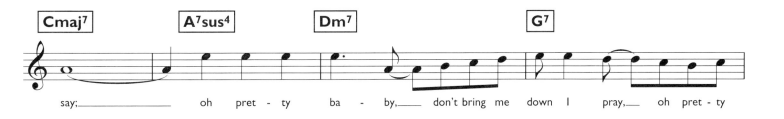

say;_____ oh pret - ty ba - by,___ don't bring me down I pray,___ oh pret - ty

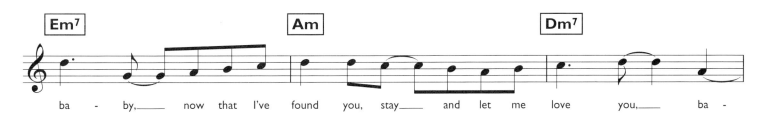

ba - by,___ now that I've found you, stay___ and let me love you,___ ba -

- by, let me love you._____

17

Cecilia

Words & Music by Paul Simon

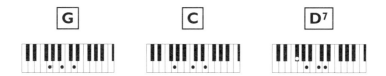

Voice: **Synth Guitar**
Rhythm: **Rock**
Tempo: ♩ = 112

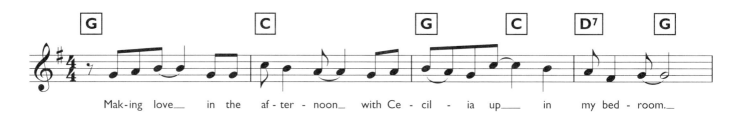

Mak-ing love in the af-ter-noon with Ce - cil - ia up in my bed - room.

I got up to wash my face, when I come back to bed some-one's tak-en my place.

Cel - ia you're break-ing my heart, you're shak-ing my con - fi - dence dai -

- ly. Oh, Ce - cil - ia, I'm down on my knees, I'm

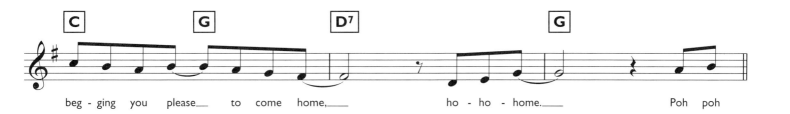

beg - ging you please___ to come home,___ ho - ho - home.___ Poh poh

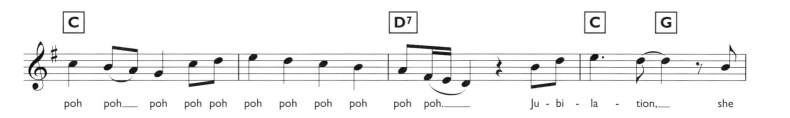

poh poh___ poh poh poh poh poh poh poh poh poh.___ Ju - bi - la - tion,___ she

loves me a - gain,___ I fall on the floor___ and I'm laugh - ing.___ Ju - bi - la - tion,___ she

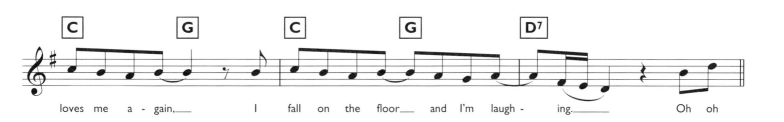

loves me a - gain,___ I fall on the floor___ and I'm laugh - ing.___ Oh oh

Repeat and fade

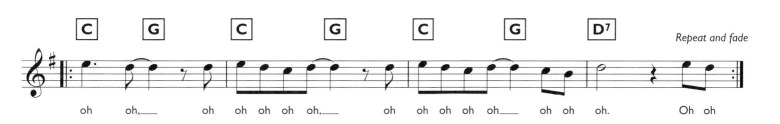

oh oh,___ oh oh oh oh oh,___ oh oh oh oh oh___ oh oh oh. Oh oh

Cracklin' Rosie

Words & Music by Neil Diamond

Voice: Saxophone
Rhythm: 8 beat
Tempo: ♩ = 118

Crack-lin' Ro - sie, get on board.___ We're gon - na ride___ till there ain't___ no more___ to

go, tak - in' it slow.___ And Lord, don't you

know, I'll have me a time___ with a poor___ man's la - dy!

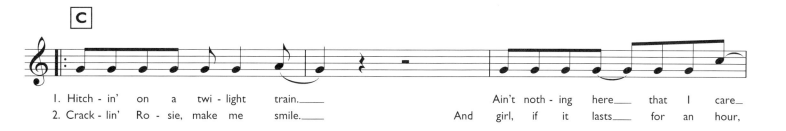

1. Hitch - in' on a twi - light train._____ Ain't noth - ing here____ that I care__
2. Crack - lin' Ro - sie, make me smile._____ And girl, if it lasts____ for an hour,

_____ to take_____ a - long, may - be a song_____
_____ that's____ al - right. We got all night_____

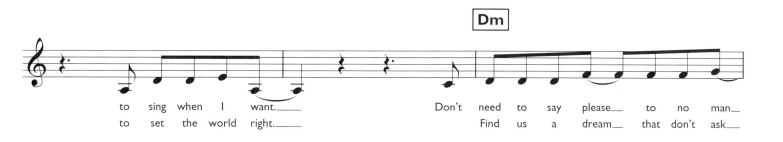

to sing when I want._____ Don't need to say please____ to no man__
to set the world right._____ Find us a dream____ that don't ask__

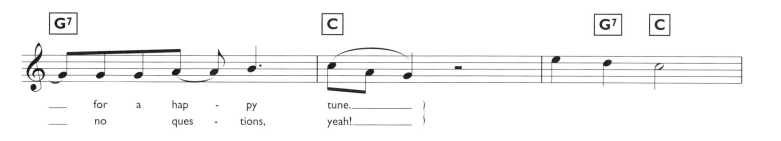

_____ for a hap - py tune._____
_____ no ques - tions, yeah!_____

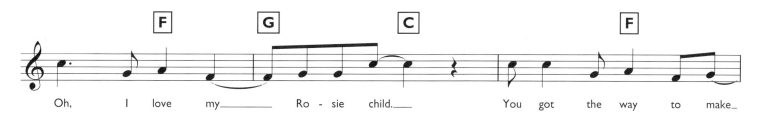

Oh, I love my_____ Ro - sie child.____ You got the way to make__

21

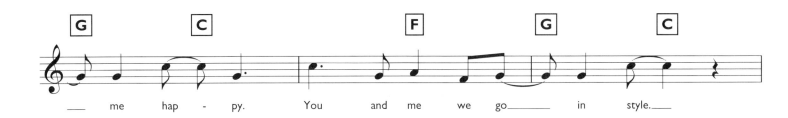

__ me hap - py. You and me we go__ in style.__

Crack - 'l - in' Rose,__ you're a store - bought wo - man, but you make me feel__ like a gui -

- tar hum - min'. So hang on to me,__ girl, our song__ keeps run - nin' on.__

__ Play it now!__ Play

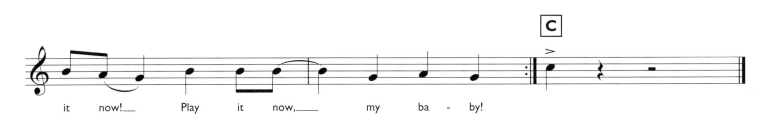

it now!__ Play it now,__ my ba - by!

Don't Let The Sun Go Down On Me

Words & Music by Elton John & Bernie Taupin

Voice: **Piano**
Rhythm: **8 Beat**
Tempo: ♩ = 66

I can't light__ no more of your dark - ness.__

All my pic - tures_____ seem to fade__ to black__ and white.__

I'm__ grow-ing tired and time stands still be - fore_____ me.__

Fro-zen here__ on the lad - der of__ my__ life.

Too late____ to save my-self____ from fall - ing.____

I____ took a chance____ and changed your way____ of life.____

____ But you mis - read

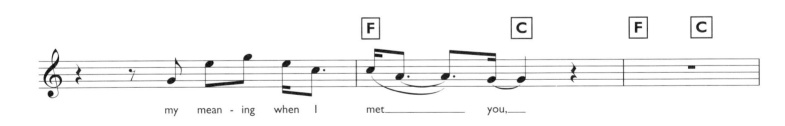

my mean - ing when I met_____ you,____

closed the door and left me blind -

-ed by____ the light._____ Don't let the sun_____ go

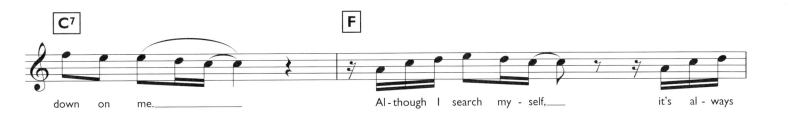

down on me._____ Al-though I search my-self,____ it's al-ways

some-one else____ I see.____ I'd just al-low a frag - ment of your

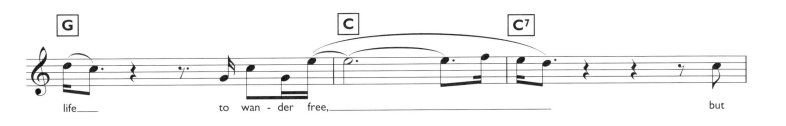

life____ to wan - der free,_____ but

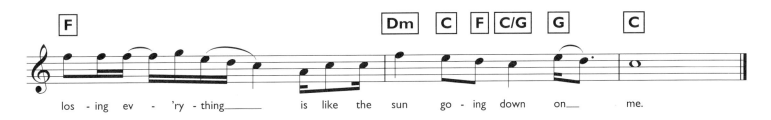

los - ing ev - 'ry-thing_____ is like the sun go - ing down on____ me.

Downtown

Words & Music by Tony Hatch

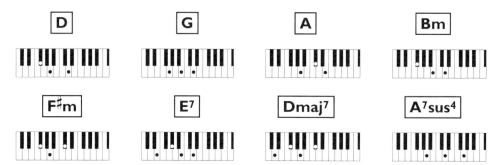

Voice: **Clarinet**
Rhythm: **Pop**
Tempo: ♩ = 108

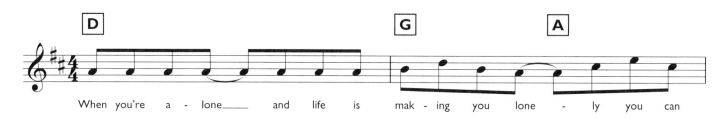

When you're a - lone____ and life is mak - ing you lone - ly you can

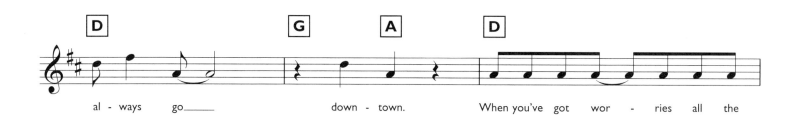

al - ways go____ down - town. When you've got wor - ries all the

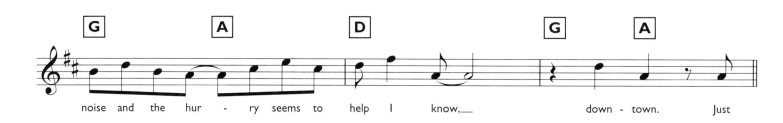

noise and the hur - ry seems to help I know,____ down - town. Just

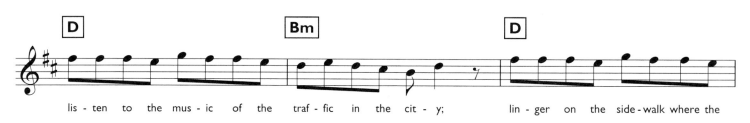

lis - ten to the mus - ic of the traf - fic in the cit - y; lin - ger on the side - walk where the

ne - on signs are pret - ty. How can you lose? The lights____ are much

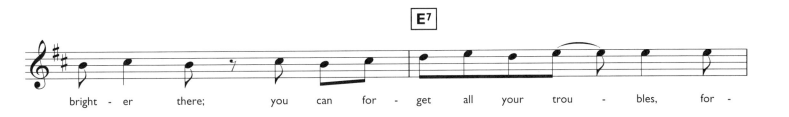

bright - er there; you can for - get all your trou - bles, for -

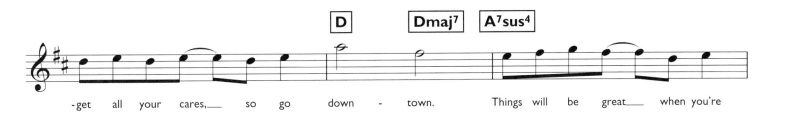

-get all your cares,____ so go down - town. Things will be great____ when you're

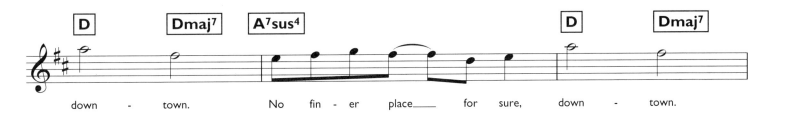

down - town. No fin - er place____ for sure, down - town.

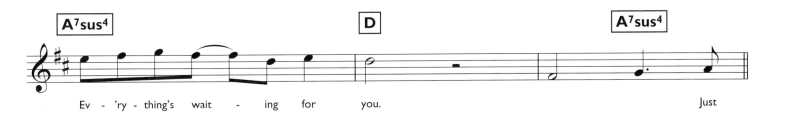

Ev - 'ry - thing's wait - ing for you. Just

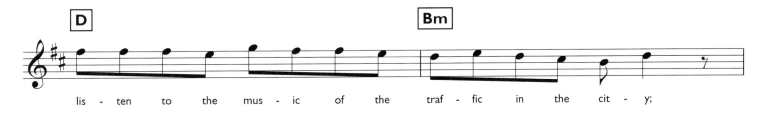

lis - ten to the mus - ic of the traf - fic in the cit - y;

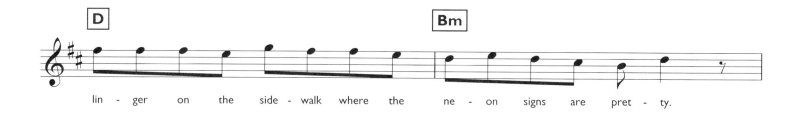

lin - ger on the side - walk where the ne - on signs are pret - ty.

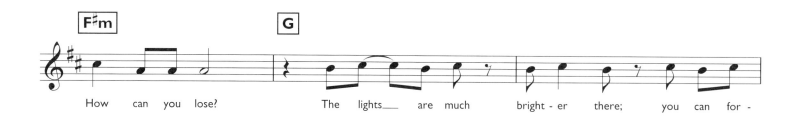

How can you lose? The lights___ are much bright - er there; you can for -

-get all your trou - bles, for - get all your cares,___ so go down - town.

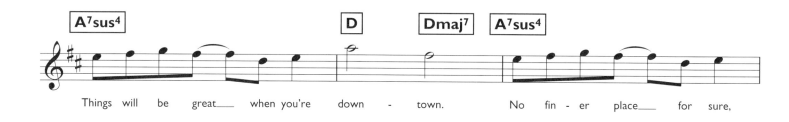

Things will be great___ when you're down - town. No fin - er place___ for sure,

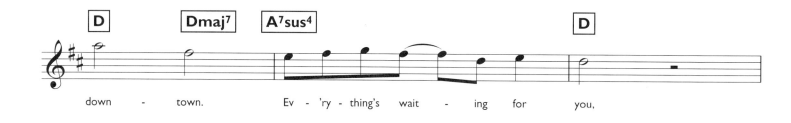

down - town. Ev - 'ry - thing's wait - ing for you,

down - town.

I Walk The Line

Words & Music by Johnny Cash

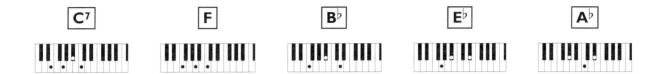

Voice: Steel guitar
Rhythm: Country
Tempo: ♩ = 108

I keep a close watch on this heart of mine.

I keep my eyes wide o - pen all the time.

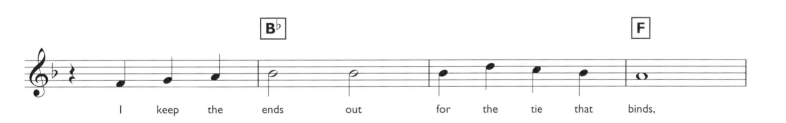

I keep the ends out for the tie that binds,

be - cause you're mine, I walk the line.

I find it ve - ry, ve - ry ea - sy to be true.

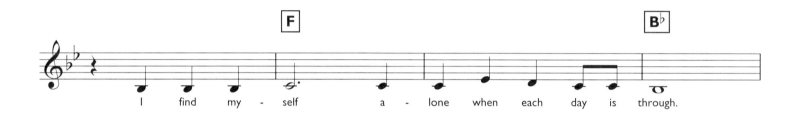

I find my - self a - lone when each day is through.

Yes I'll ad - mit that I'm_____ a fool for you,

be - cause you're mine, I walk the line.

As sure as night is dark and day is

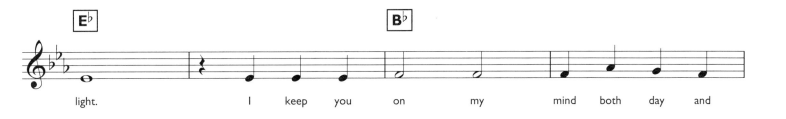

light. I keep you on my mind both day and

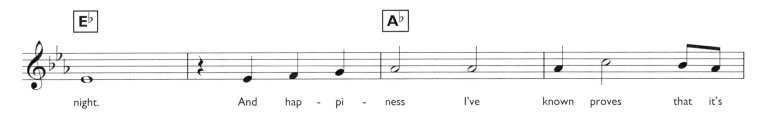

night. And hap - pi - ness I've known proves that it's

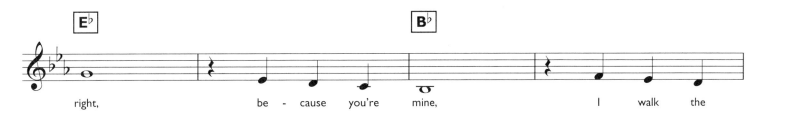

right, be - cause you're mine, I walk the

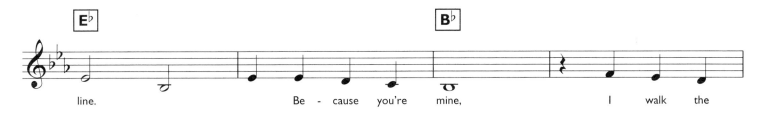

line. Be - cause you're mine, I walk the

line.

Everybody's Talkin'

Words & Music by Fred Neil

Voice: **Guitar**
Rhythm: **8 beat**
Tempo: ♩ = 120

Ev - 'ry-bod- y's talk - in' at_____ me, I don't hear a word they're say - in',

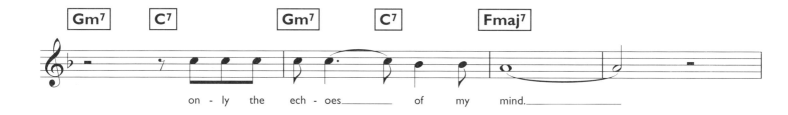

on - ly the ech -oes_____ of my mind.

Peo - ple stop and stare_____ and I can't see their fac - es,_____

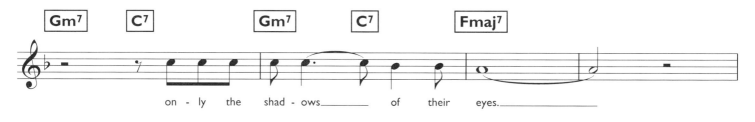

on - ly the shad - ows_____ of their eyes._____

I'm go - in' where the sun keeps shin - in'_____ through the pour - in'_____ rain.__

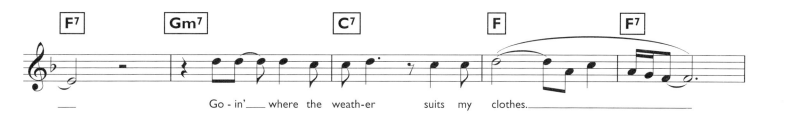

__ Go - in'___ where the weath-er suits my clothes._____

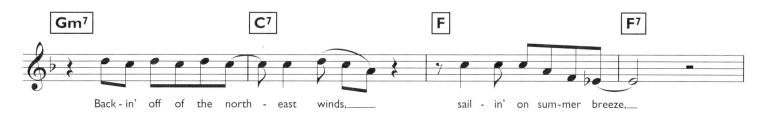

Back - in' off of the north - east winds,_____ sail - in' on sum-mer breeze,__

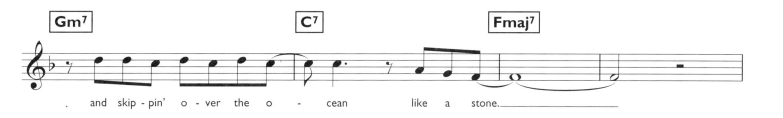

. and skip - pin' o - ver the o - cean like a stone._____

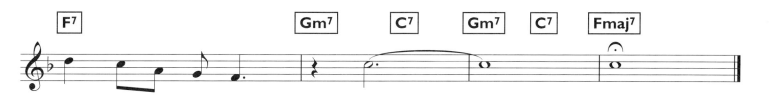

The First Cut Is The Deepest

Words & Music by Cat Stevens

Voice: **Synth Lead**
Rhythm: **Rock**
Tempo: ♩ = 96

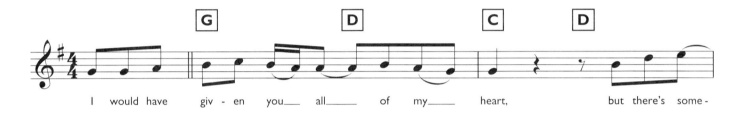

I would have giv-en you___ all___ of my___ heart, but there's some-

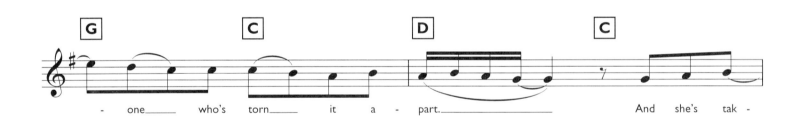

-one___ who's torn___ it a-part.___ And she's tak-

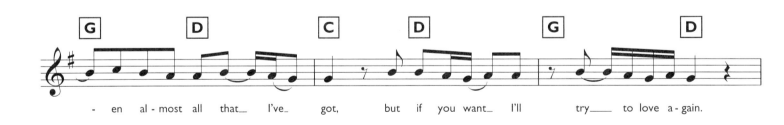

-en al-most all that___ I've___ got, but if you want___ I'll try___ to love a-gain.

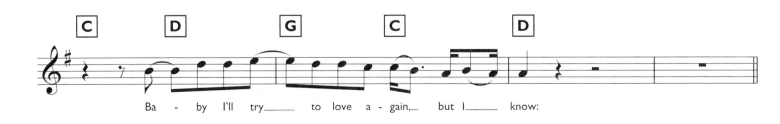

Ba- by I'll try___ to love a-gain, but I___ know:

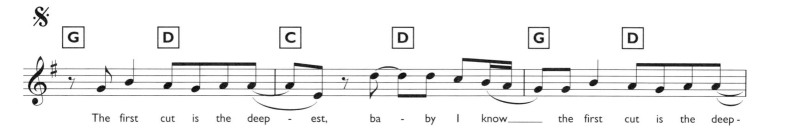

The first cut is the deep - est, ba - by I know___ the first cut is the deep -

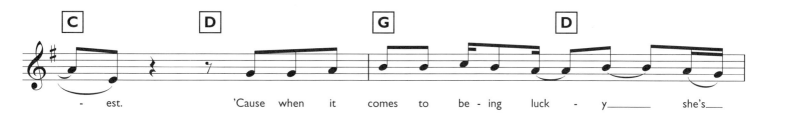

- est. 'Cause when it comes to be - ing luck - y___ she's___

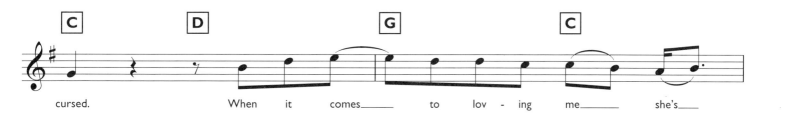

cursed. When it comes___ to lov - ing me___ she's___

worst,_____ but when it comes to be - ing loved she's_____

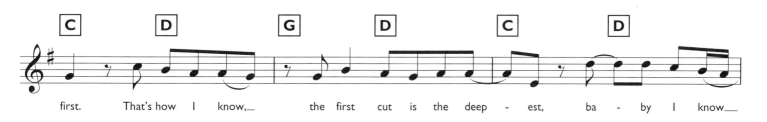

first. That's how I know,___ the first cut is the deep - est, ba - by I know___

To Coda

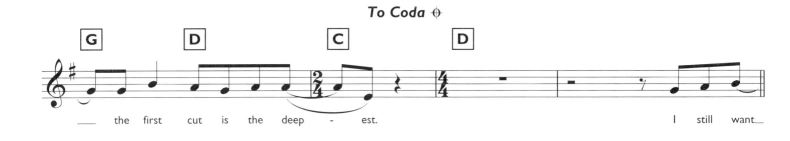

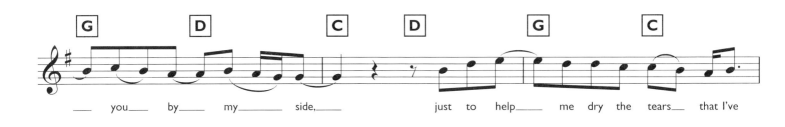

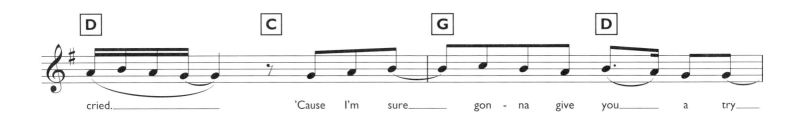

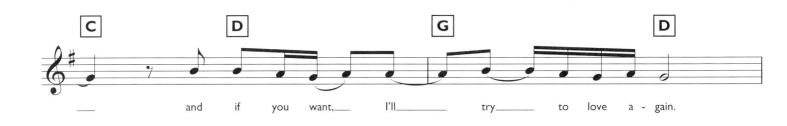

D.S. al Coda

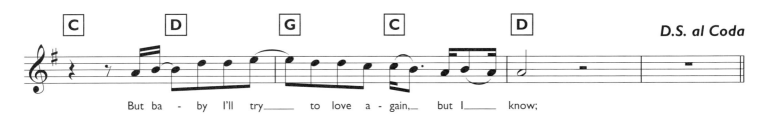

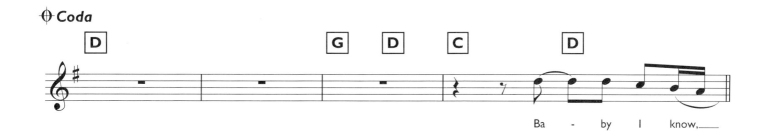

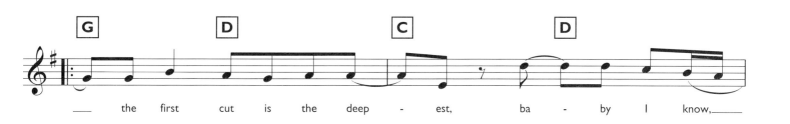

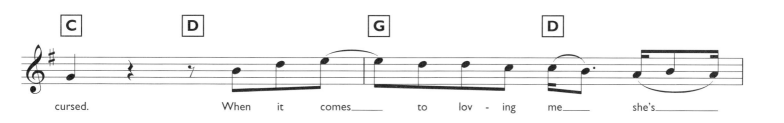

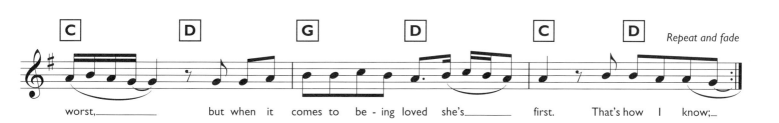

37

Georgia On My Mind

Words by Stuart Gorrell
Music by Hoagy Carmichael

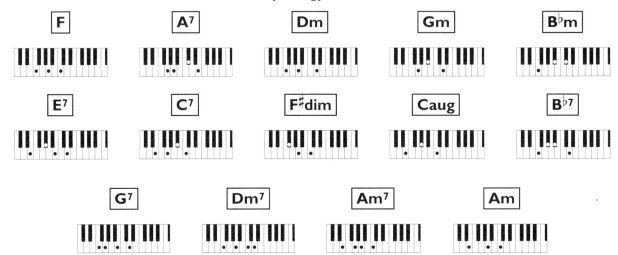

Voice: **Flute**
Rhythm: **Soul Ballad**
Tempo: ♩ = 66

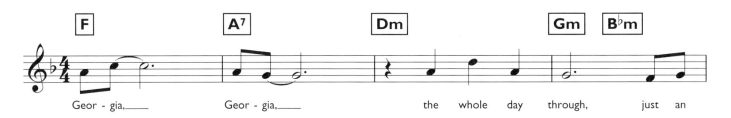

Geor - gia,____ Geor - gia,____ the whole day through, just an

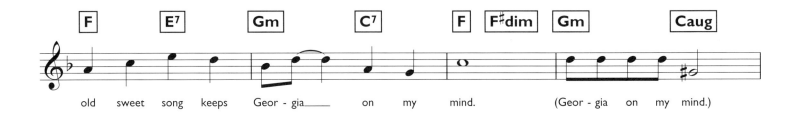

old sweet song keeps Geor - gia____ on my mind. (Geor - gia on my mind.)

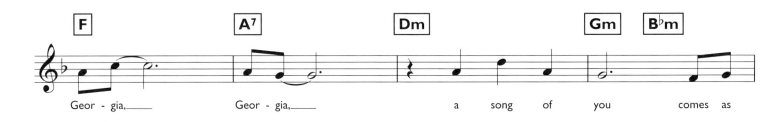

Geor - gia,____ Geor - gia,____ a song of you comes as

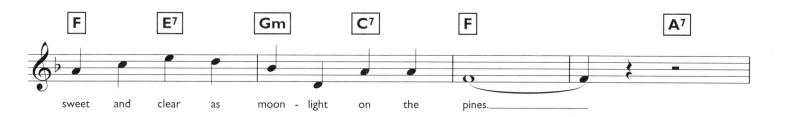

sweet and clear as moon - light on the pines._____

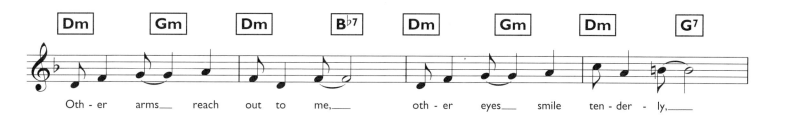

Oth - er arms____ reach out to me,____ oth - er eyes____ smile ten - der - ly,____

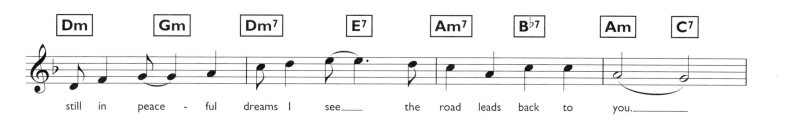

still in peace - ful dreams I see____ the road leads back to you.____

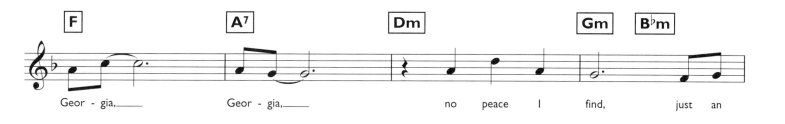

Geor - gia,____ Geor - gia,____ no peace I find, just an

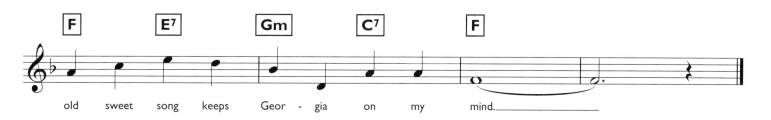

old sweet song keeps Geor - gia on my mind.____

Great Balls Of Fire

Words & Music by Otis Blackwell & Jack Hammer

Voice: **Electric guitar**
Rhythm: **Rock 'n' Roll**
Tempo: ♩ = 148

You shake my nerves and you rat-tle my brain.__ Too much love drives a man in-sane.__

You broke my will, but what a thrill. Good-ness gra-cious, Great__ Balls Of Fire!__

I laughed at love 'cause I thought it was fun - ny. You came a-long and moved__ me, hon-ey.

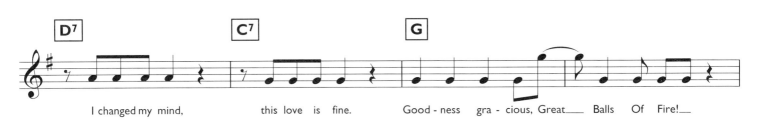

I changed my mind, this love is fine. Good-ness gra-cious, Great__ Balls Of Fire!__

Kiss me, ba - by. Oh, oh! It feels good.

Hold me, ba - by. I want to love you like a lov - er should.__

You're fine,__ so kind.__ I'm gon - na tell the world that you're mine, mine, mine, mine.

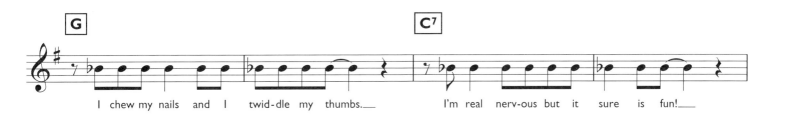

I chew my nails and I twid - dle my thumbs.__ I'm real nerv-ous but it sure is fun!__

Oh, ba - by, you're driv - in' me cra - zy. Good - ness gra - cious, Great__ Balls Of Fire!__

Oh, ba - by, you're driv - in' me cra - zy. Good - ness gra - cious, Great__ Balls Of Fire!__

Heartbeat

Words & Music by Bob Montgomery & Norman Petty

Voice: **Piano**
Rhythm: **Rock 'n' Roll**
Tempo: ♩ = 140

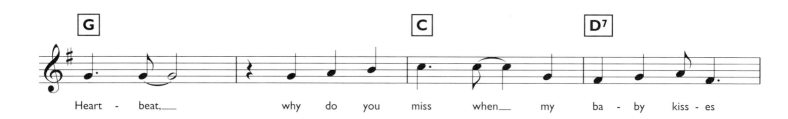

Heart - beat,___ why do you miss when___ my ba - by kiss - es

me?

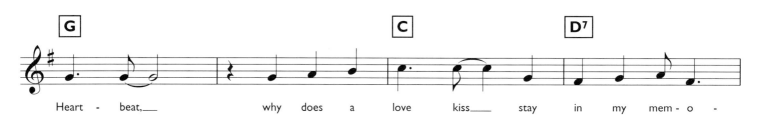

Heart - beat,___ why does a love kiss___ stay in my mem - o -

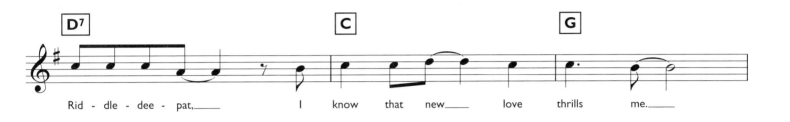

It's Not Unusual

Words & Music by Gordon Mills & Les Reed

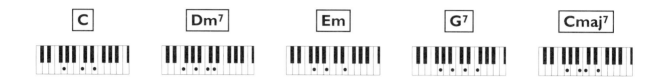

Voice: **Organ**
Rhythm: **8 beat**
Tempo: ♩ = 144

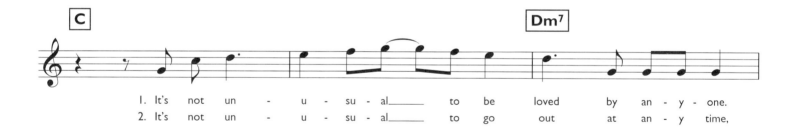

1. It's not un - u - su - al_____ to be loved by an - y - one.
2. It's not un - u - su - al_____ to go out at an - y time,

It's not un - u - su - al_____ to have
but when I see you out_____ and a -

fun with an - y - one._____ But when I

Dm⁷

see you | hang - ing | a - bout_____ | with | an - y - one,_____
ev - er | wan - na | be loved_____ | by | an - y - one,_____

G⁷   1.   C

it's not un - u - su - al_____ to see me cry,_____
it's not un - u - su - al,_____ it

Dm⁷   G⁷

I wan - na die._____

2.
C   Dm⁷

hap - pens ev - 'ry day, no mat - ter what____ you say,

G⁷

you'll find it hap - pens_____ all the

C

time._____ Love will nev - er do

what you want__ it to.   Why can't this cra - zy love__ be

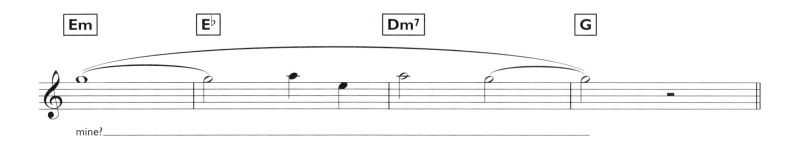

mine?_____

Lady Madonna

Words & Music by John Lennon & Paul McCartney

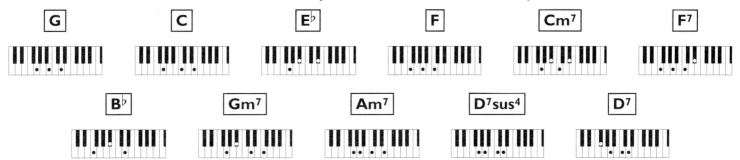

Voice: **Violin**
Rhythm: **Soft Rock 1**
Tempo: ♩ = 92

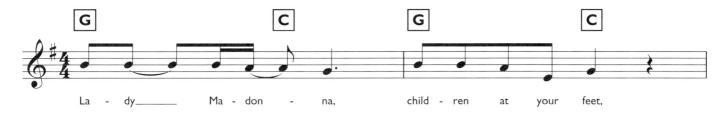

La - dy_____ Ma - don - na, child - ren at your feet,

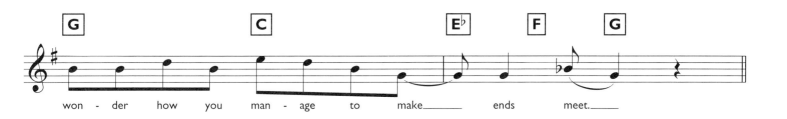

won - der how you man - age to make_____ ends meet._____

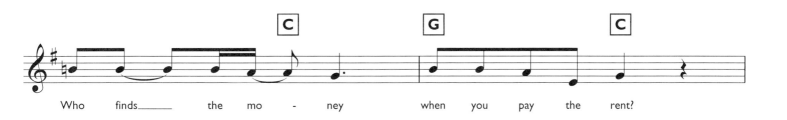

Who finds_____ the mo - ney when you pay the rent?

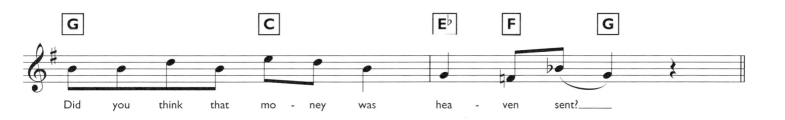

Did you think that mo - ney was hea - ven sent?_____

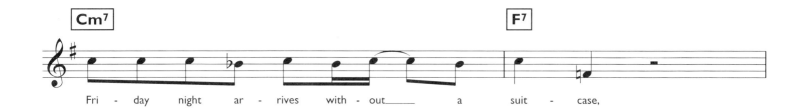

Fri - day night ar - rives with - out____ a suit - case,

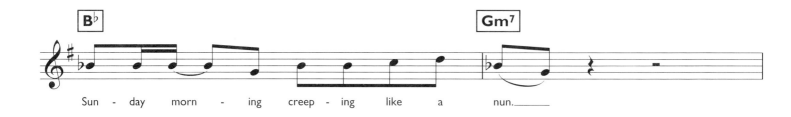

Sun - day morn - ing creep - ing like a nun.____

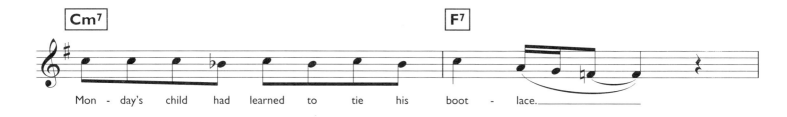

Mon - day's child had learned to tie his boot - lace.____

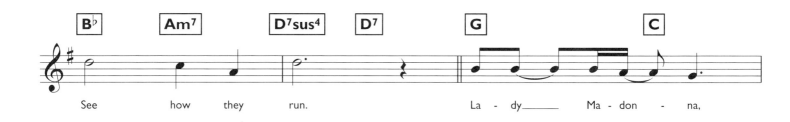

See how they run. La - dy____ Ma - don - na,

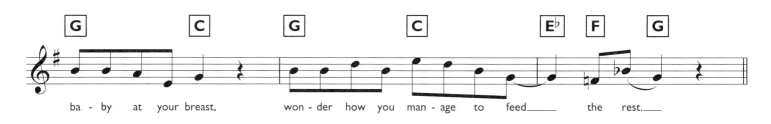

ba - by at your breast, won - der how you man - age to feed____ the rest.____

Tues - day af - ter - noon___ is nev - er end - ing,

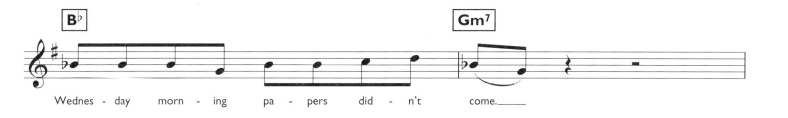

Wednes - day morn - ing pa - pers did - n't come.___

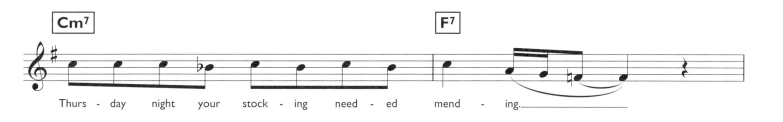

Thurs - day night your stock - ing need - ed mend - ing.___

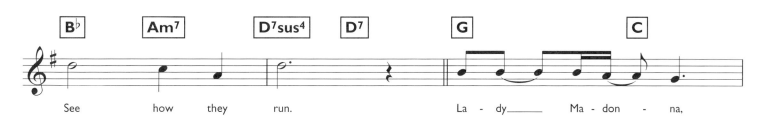

See how they run. La - dy___ Ma - don - na,

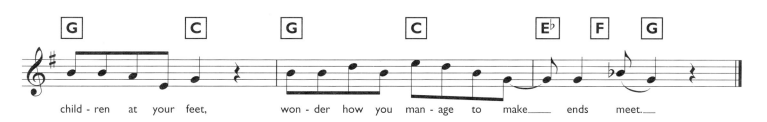

child - ren at your feet, won - der how you man - age to make___ ends meet.___

Knowing Me, Knowing You

Words & Music by Benny Andersson, Stig Anderson & Björn Ulvaeus

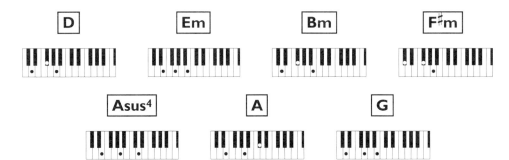

Voice: **Flute**
Rhythm: **8 beat**
Tempo: ♩ = 120

No more___ care - free___ laugh - ter._____

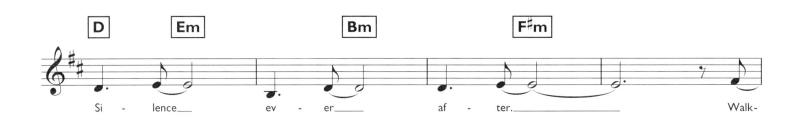

Si - lence___ ev - er___ af - ter._____ Walk-

- ing through an emp - ty house,___ tears in my eyes.___

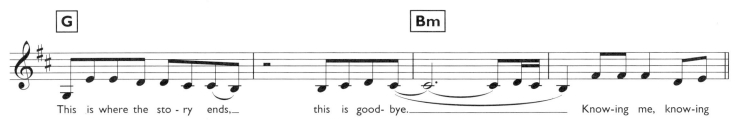

This is where the sto - ry ends,___ this is good- bye._____ Know-ing me, know-ing

you, there is noth - ing we can do.____ Know - ing me know - ing

you, we just have to face it, this time____ we're through.

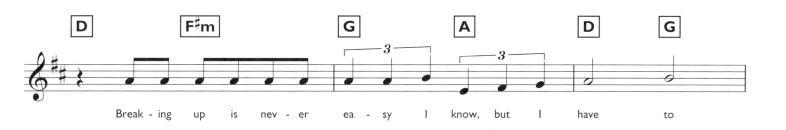

Break - ing up is nev - er ea - sy I know, but I have to

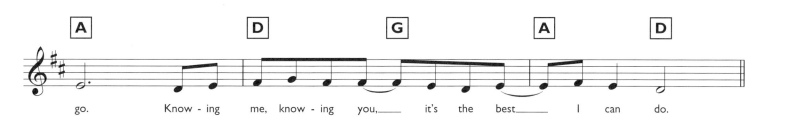

go. Know - ing me, know - ing you,____ it's the best____ I can do.

Magic Moments

Words by Hal David
Music by Burt Bacharach

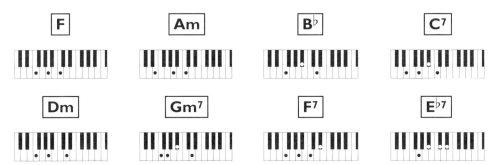

Voice: **Horn**
Rhythm: **Swing**
Tempo: ♩ = 100

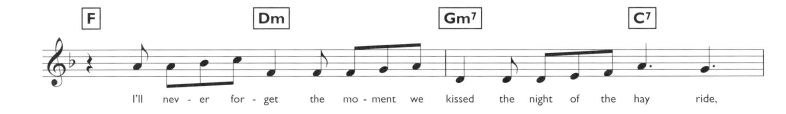

I'll nev-er for-get the mo-ment we kissed the night of the hay ride,

the way that we hugged to try and keep warm while tak-ing a sleigh ride.

Ma - gic mo - ments, mem - 'ries we've been

shar - ing. Ma - gic mo - ments,

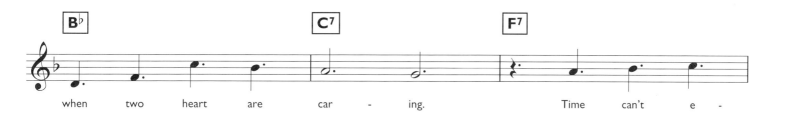

when two heart are car - ing. Time can't e -

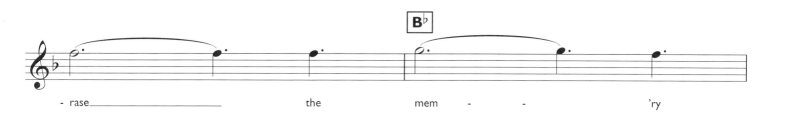

- rase the mem - - 'ry

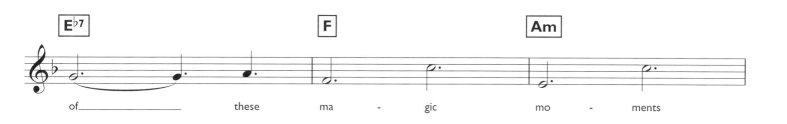

of these ma - gic mo - ments

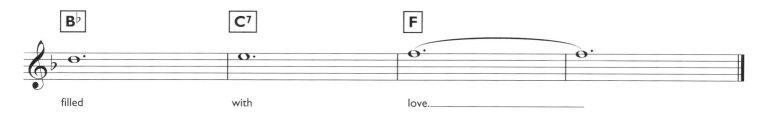

filled with love.

Moon River

Words by Johnny Mercer
Music by Henry Mancini

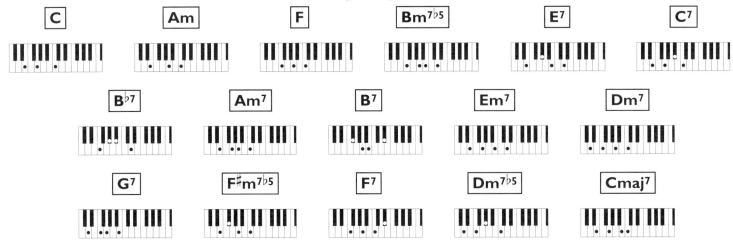

Voice: **Flute**
Rhythm: **Waltz**
Tempo: ♩ = 78

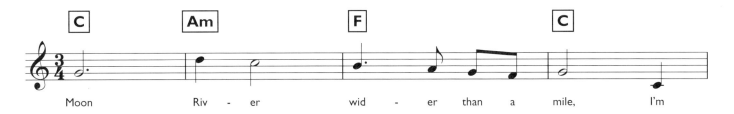

Moon Riv - er wid - er than a mile, I'm

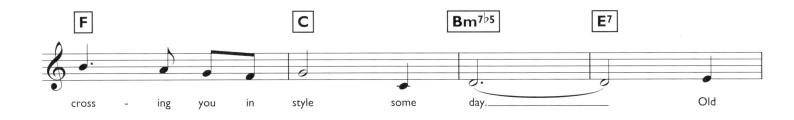

cross - ing you in style some day.___ Old

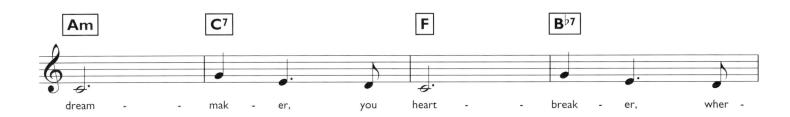

dream - - mak - er, you heart - - break - er, wher -

ev - er you're go - in',_____ I'm go - in'_____ your way.

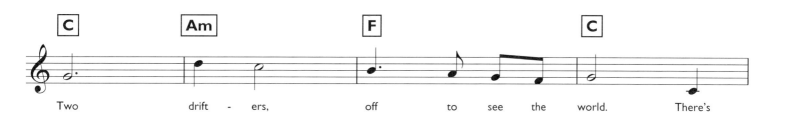

Two drift - ers, off to see the world. There's

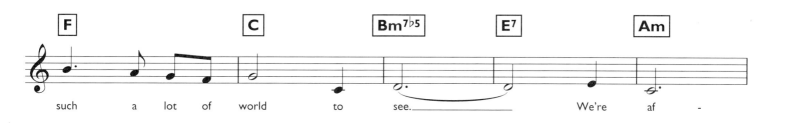

such a lot of world to see._____ We're af -

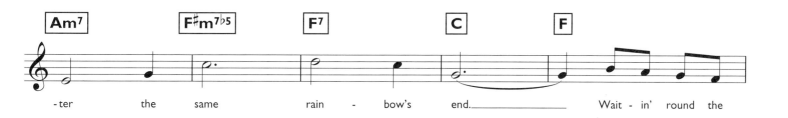

-ter the same rain - bow's end._____ Wait - in' round the

bend,_____ my Huck - le - ber - ry friend, Moon

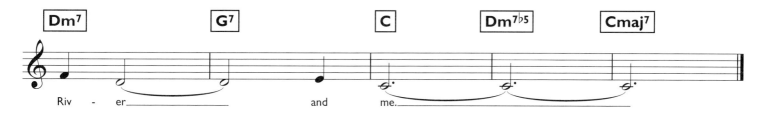

Riv - er_____ and me._____

Oh, Pretty Woman

Words & Music by Roy Orbison & Bill Dees

Voice: **Saxophone**
Rhythm: **Rock 'n' Roll**
Tempo: ♩ = 116

Pret - ty

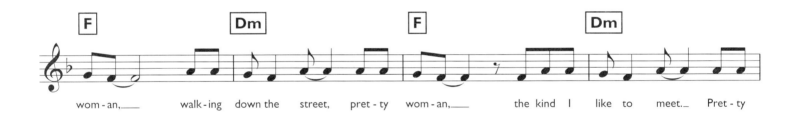

wom-an,____ walk-ing down the street, pret-ty wom-an,____ the kind I like to meet.__ Pret-ty

wom - an,_____ I don't be - lieve you,_____ you're not the

truth._____ No - one could look as good as you._____

Positively 4th Street

Words & Music by Bob Dylan

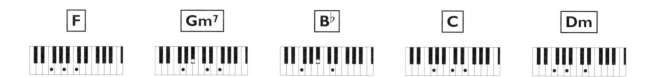

Voice: **Electric Piano**
Rhythm: **Soft Rock**
Tempo: ♩ = 114

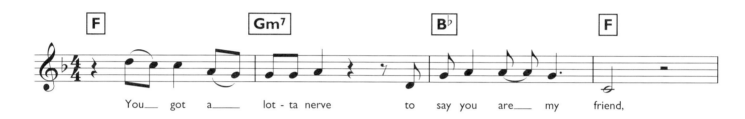

You__ got a__ lot-ta nerve to say you are__ my friend,

when I was down you just stood there grin - ning.

You got a__ lot-ta nerve__ to say you got-ta help-ing__ hand to lend.

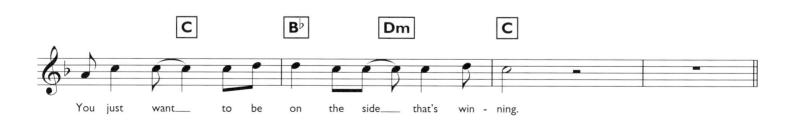

You just want__ to be on the side__ that's win-ning.

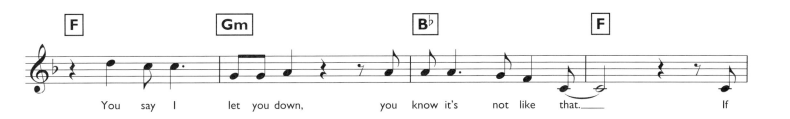

You say I let you down, you know it's not like that.____ If

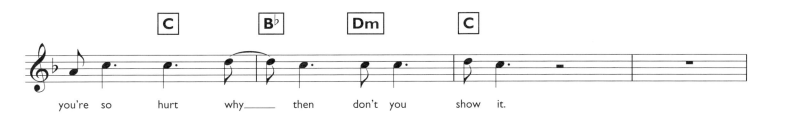

you're so hurt why____ then don't you show it.

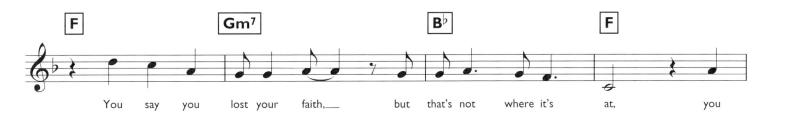

You say you lost your faith,____ but that's not where it's at, you

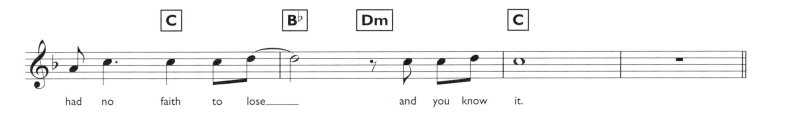

had no faith to lose____ and you know it.

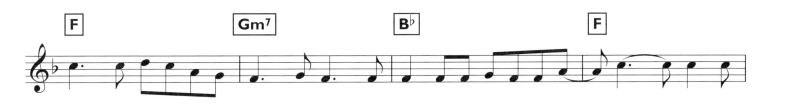

Release Me

Words & Music by Eddie Miller, Dub Williams & Robert Yount

Voice: **Clarinet**
Rhythm: **Soft Rock**
Tempo: ♩ = 110

Please re - lease me, let me go,_____ for

I don't love you an - y - more. To

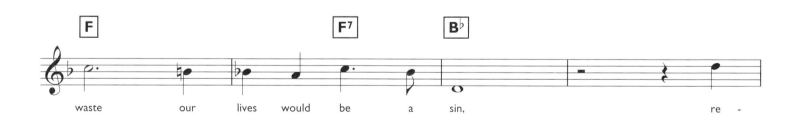

waste our lives would be a sin, re -

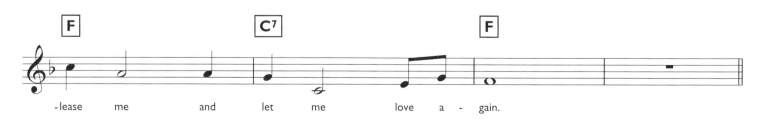

-lease me and let me love a - gain.

Please . . . . re - lease me, can't you see?

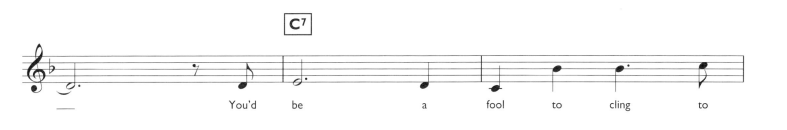

You'd be a fool to cling to

me. To live a lie would bring us

pain, so re - lease me and

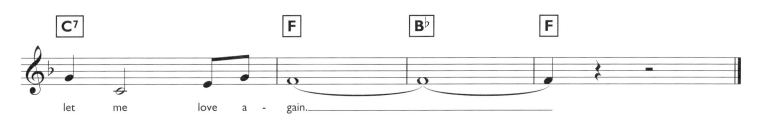

let me love a - gain.

She

Words by Herbert Kretzmer
Music by Charles Aznavour

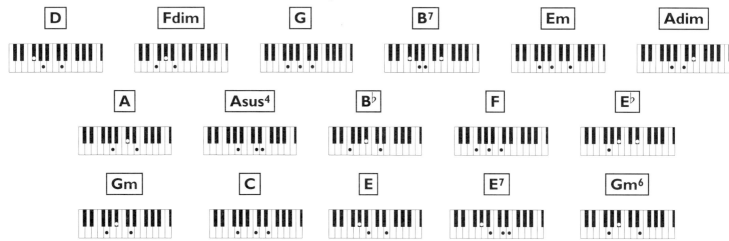

Voice: **Saxophone**
Rhythm: **Ballad**
Tempo: ♩ = 65

She____ may be the face I can't for - get,____ a trace of plea - sure or re -

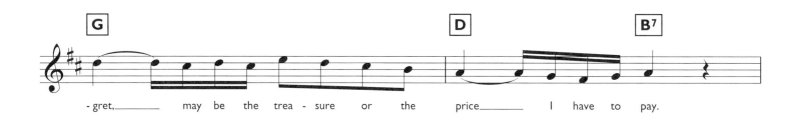

- gret,____ may be the trea - sure or the price____ I have to pay.

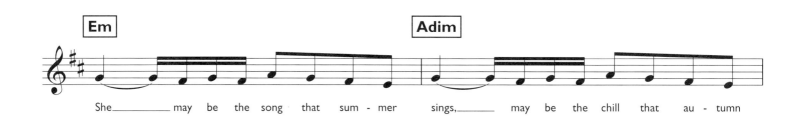

She____ may be the song that sum - mer sings,____ may be the chill that au - tumn

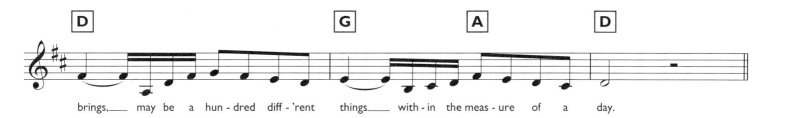

brings,___ may be a hun-dred diff-'rent things___ with-in the meas-ure of a day.

She___ may be the beau-ty or the beast,___ may be the fa-mine or the

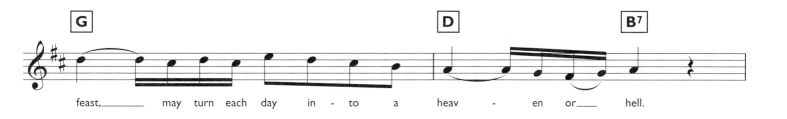

feast,___ may turn each day in-to a heav-en or___ hell.

She___ may be the mir-ror of my dreams___ a smile re-flect-ed in a

To Coda ⊕

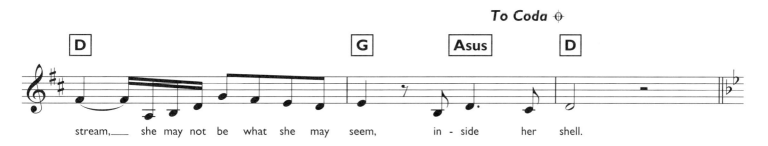

stream,___ she may not be what she may seem, in-side her shell.

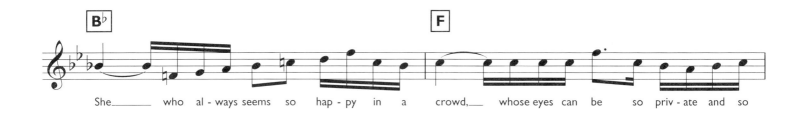

She_____ who al-ways seems so hap-py in a crowd,_____ whose eyes can be so priv-ate and so

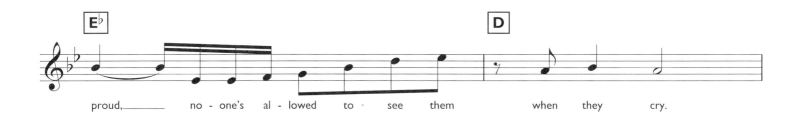

proud,_____ no - one's al - lowed to · see them when they cry.

She_____ may be the love that can-not hope to last,_____ may come to me from shad-ows of the

D.S. al Coda

past_____ that I'll re - mem - ber till the day I die.

𝄋 Coda

shell.   She.

64

(Sittin' On) The Dock Of The Bay

Words & Music by Otis Redding & Steve Cropper

Voice: **Rock Organ**
Rhythm: **Country Rock**
Tempo: ♩ = 100

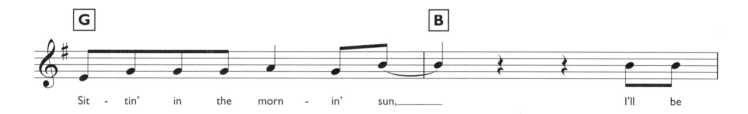

Sit - tin' in the morn - in' sun,_____ I'll be

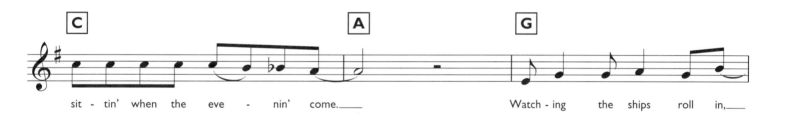

sit - tin' when the eve - nin' come._____ Watch - ing the ships roll in,_____

_____ then I watch 'em roll a - way a - gain._____ I'm

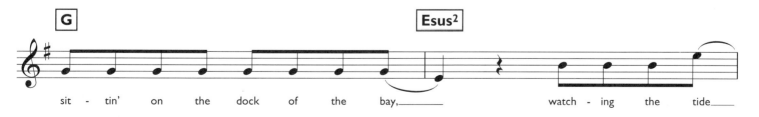

sit - tin' on the dock of the bay,_____ watch - ing the tide_____

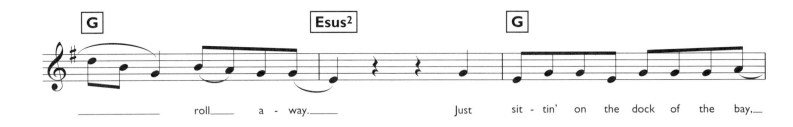

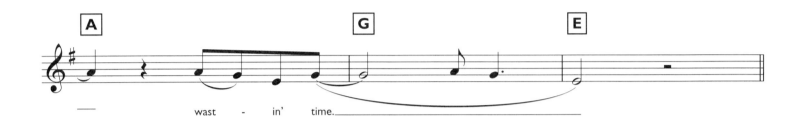

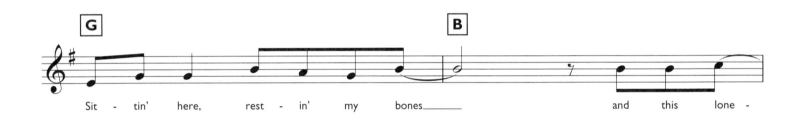

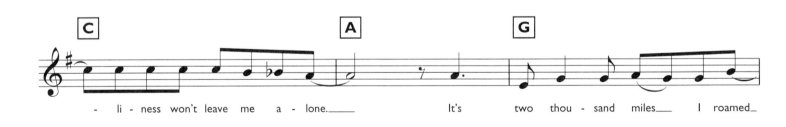

66

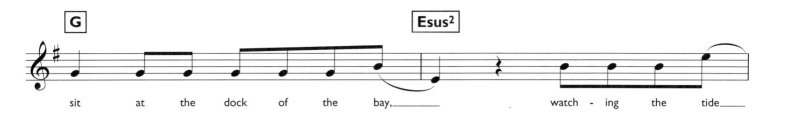

sit   at   the   dock   of   the   bay,_____   watch - ing   the   tide_____

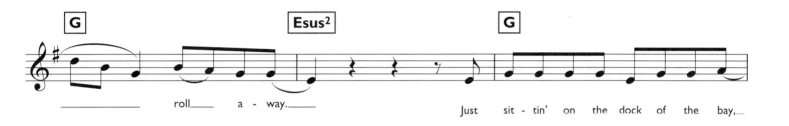

_____   roll____   a - way.____   Just   sit - tin'   on   the   dock   of   the   bay,___

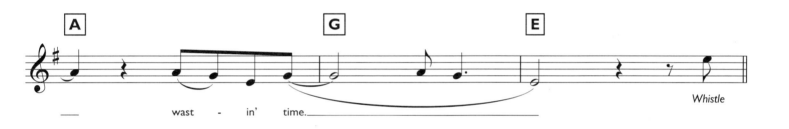

___   wast - in'   time._____   *Whistle*

Repeat and fade

Smoke Gets In Your Eyes

Words by Otto Harbach
Music by Jerome Kern

Voice: **Clarinet**
Rhythm: **Ballad**
Tempo: ♩ = 76

They asked me how I knew my true love was

true._____ I of course re - plied some - thing here in -

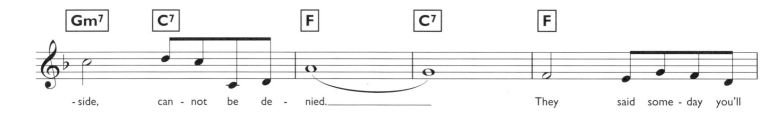

- side, can - not be de - nied._____ They said some - day you'll

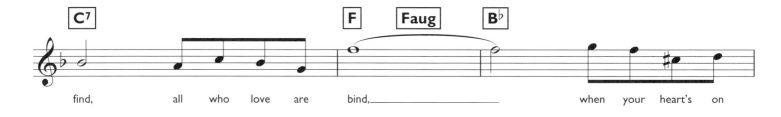

find, all who love are bind,_____ when your heart's on

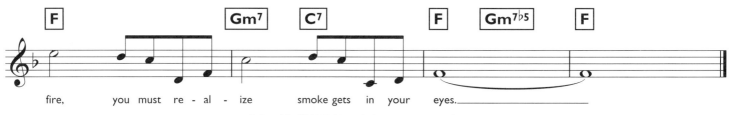

fire, you must re - al - ize smoke gets in your eyes._____

Somethin' Stupid

Words & Music by C. Carson Parks

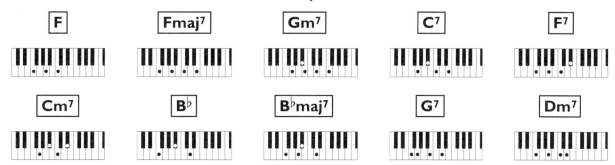

Voice: **Flute**
Rhythm: **Pop Ballad**
Tempo: ♩ = 100

I know I stand in line un - til you think you have some time to spend an eve - nin' with me.___

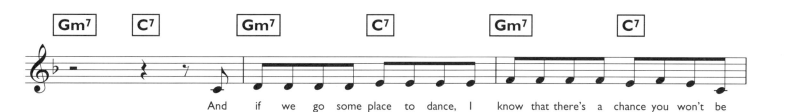

And if we go some place to dance, I know that there's a chance you won't be

leav - in' with me.___ Then af - ter - wards we drop in - to a

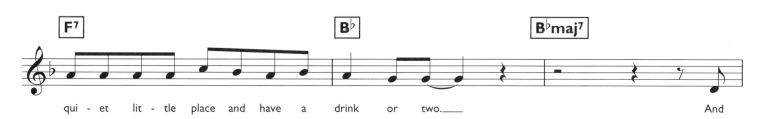

qui - et lit - tle place and have a drink or two.___ And

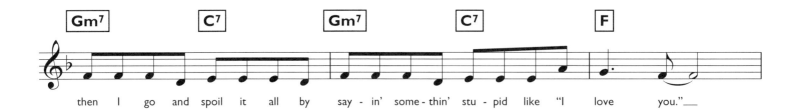

then I go and spoil it all by say-in' some-thin' stu-pid like "I love you."___

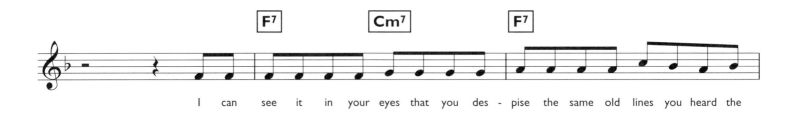

I can see it in your eyes that you des-pise the same old lines you heard the

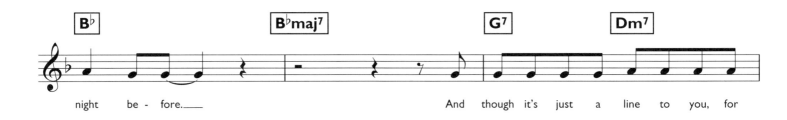

night be-fore.___ And though it's just a line to you, for

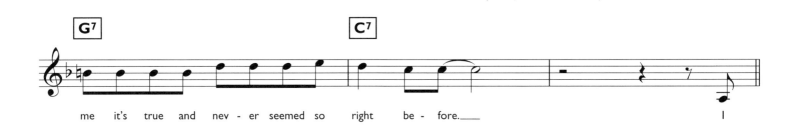

me it's true and nev-er seemed so right be-fore.___ I

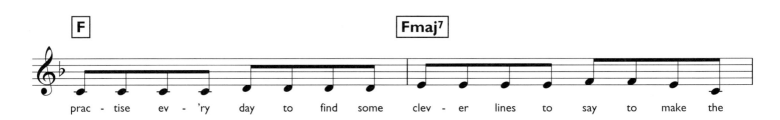

prac-tise ev-'ry day to find some clev-er lines to say to make the

mean - ing come through._____ But

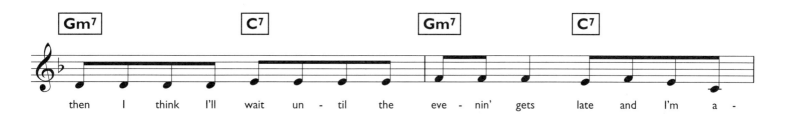

then I think I'll wait un - til the eve - nin' gets late and I'm a -

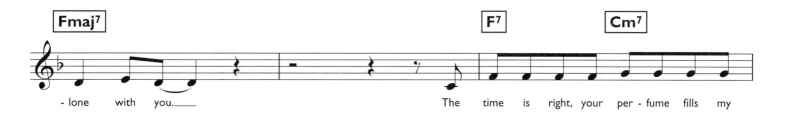

- lone with you._____ The time is right, your per - fume fills my

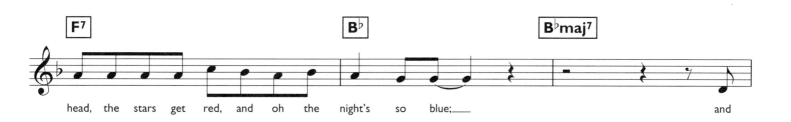

head, the stars get red, and oh the night's so blue;____ and

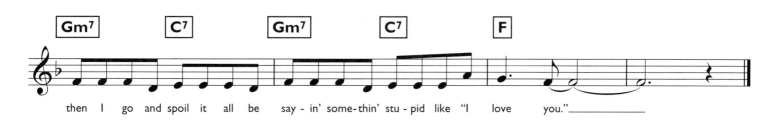

then I go and spoil it all be say - in' some - thin' stu - pid like "I love you."_____

Suspicious Minds

Words & Music by Francis Zambon

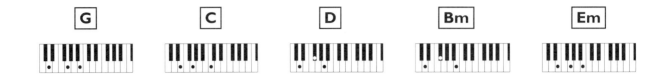

Voice: Alto Saxophone
Rhythm: Love Ballad
Tempo: ♩ = 100

That's Amore

Words & Music by Harry Warren & Jack Brooks

Voice: **Accordian**
Rhythm: **Waltz**
Tempo: ♩ = 160

When the moon hits your eye like a big piz - za

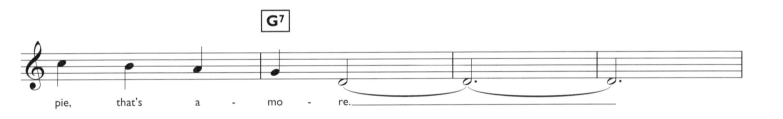

pie, that's a - mo - re.

When the world seems to shine like you've had too much

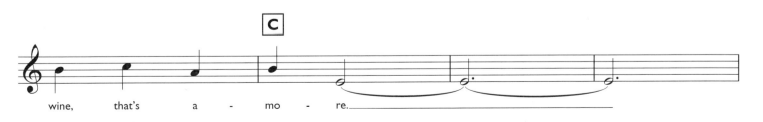

wine, that's a - mo - re.

Bells will ring, ting - a - ling - a - ling, ting - a - ling - a - ling, and you'll

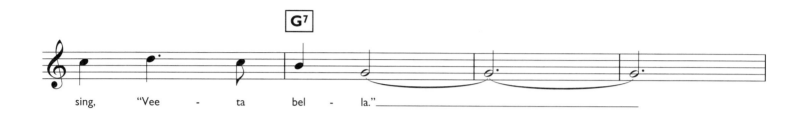

sing, "Vee - ta bel - la."

Hearts will play tip - py - tip - py - tay, tip - py tip - py tay like a

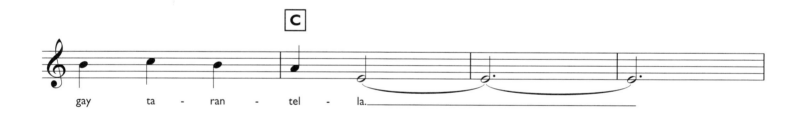

gay ta - ran - tel - la.

When the stars make you drool just like pas - ta fa -

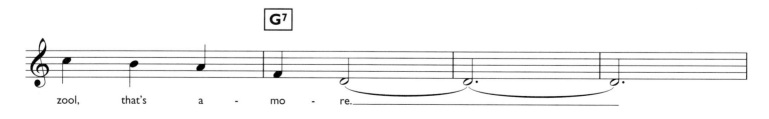

zool, that's a - mo - re.

When you dance down the street with a cloud at your

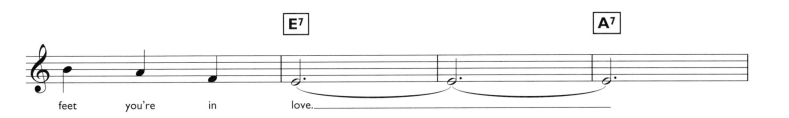

feet you're in love.

When you walk in a dream but you know you're not

dream - ing, sig - no - - ré.

Scuz - za me, but you see, back in old Na - po -

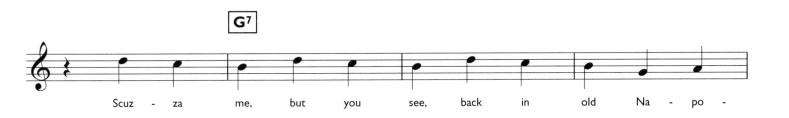

- li, that's a - mo - re.

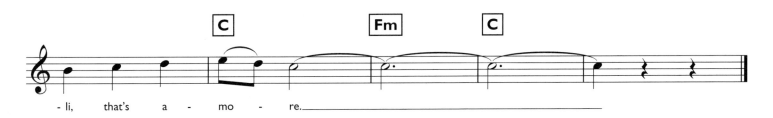

Truly

Words & Music by Lionel Richie

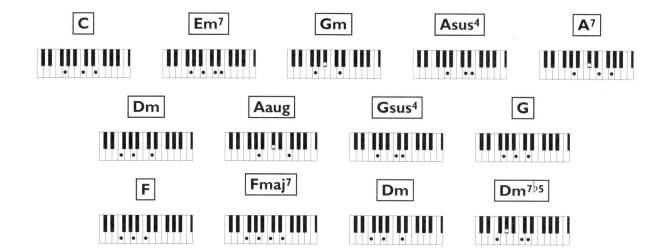

Voice: **Piano**
Rhythm: **8 beat**
Tempo: ♩ = 68

1. Girl, tell me only this: that I have your heart for
2. Now, I need to tell you this: there's no other love like

al - ways, and you want me by your side whis - per - ing the
your love, and I, as long as I live, I'll give you all the

words "I'll al - ways love you."
joy my heart and soul can give.

And for - ev - er
Let me hold you;

I will be your lov - er; and I know if you real - ly
I need to have you near me; and I feel with you in my

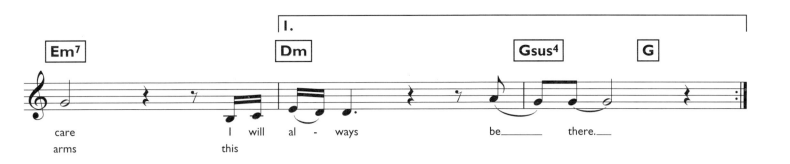

care
arms

I will al - ways
this

be_____ there.____

love will___ last for - ev - er, be - cause I'm tru - ly,_____ tru - ly in

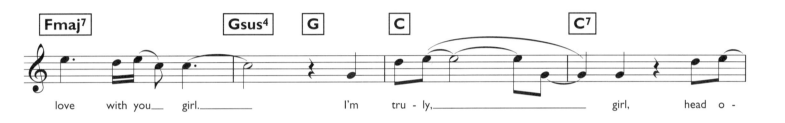

love with you___ girl._____ I'm tru - ly,_____ girl, head o -

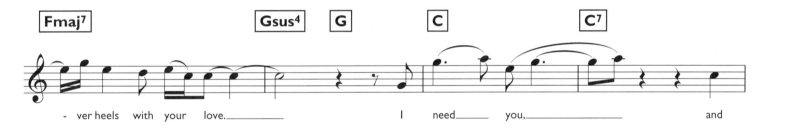

- ver heels with your love._____ I need___ you,_____ and

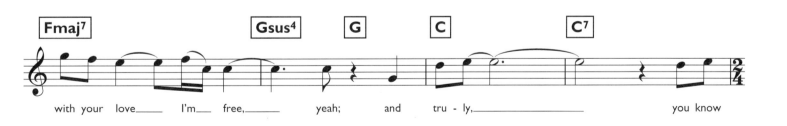

with your love_____ I'm___ free,_____ yeah; and tru - ly,_____ you know

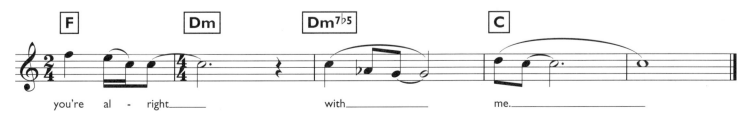

you're al - right_____ with_____ me.____

Unchained Melody

Words by Hy Zaret
Music by Alex North

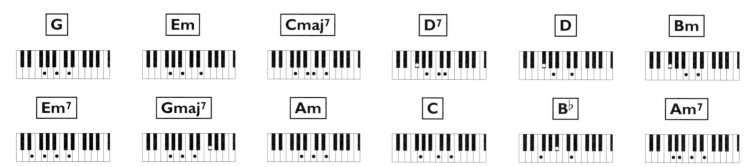

Voice: **Trumpet**
Rhythm: **Ballad**
Tempo: ♩ = 96

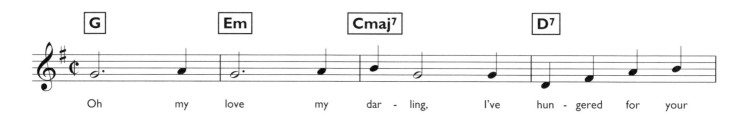

Oh my love my dar - ling, I've hun - gered for your

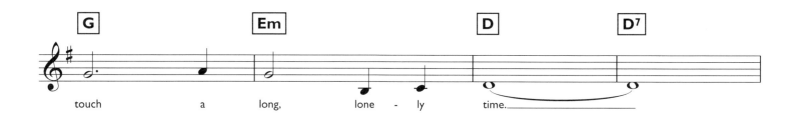

touch a long, lone - ly time.

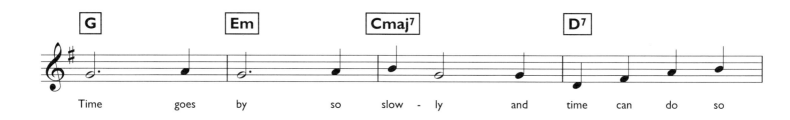

Time goes by so slow - ly and time can do so

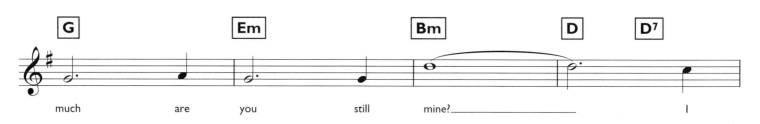

much are you still mine? I

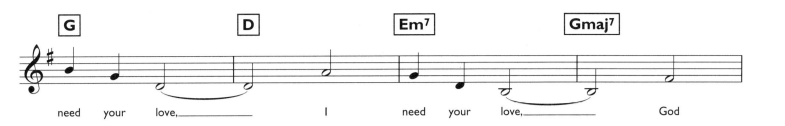

need your love,_____ I need your love,_____ God

speed your love_____ to me!_____

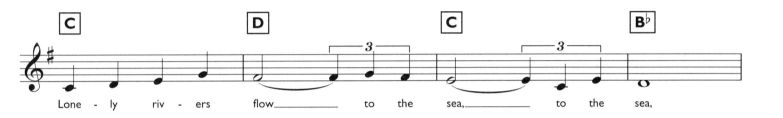

Lone - ly riv - ers flow_____ to the sea,_____ to the sea,

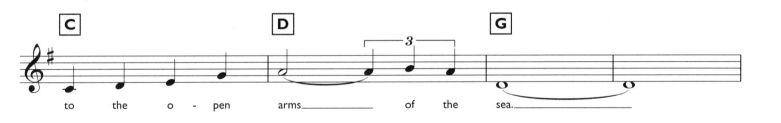

to the o - pen arms_____ of the sea._____

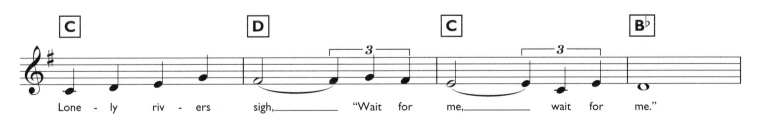

Lone - ly riv - ers sigh,_____ "Wait for me,_____ wait for me."

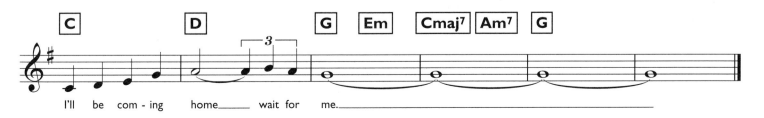

I'll be com - ing home_____ wait for me._____

Vincent

Words & Music by Don McLean

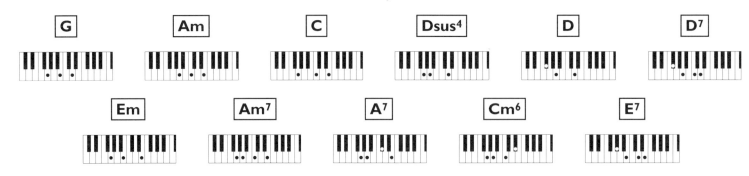

Voice: Accoustic guitar
Rhythm: Ballad
Tempo: ♩ = 90

Star - ry, star - ry night, paint your pal - ette blue and grey,

look out on a sum-mer's day with eyes that know the dark-ness in my soul. Shad-ows on the

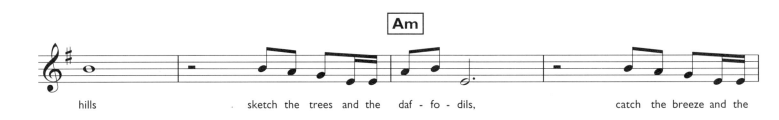

hills sketch the trees and the daf-fo-dils, catch the breeze and the

win - ter chills in col - ours on the snow - y lin - en land. Now I un-der-

-stand ... what you tried to say to me, how you suf-fered for your

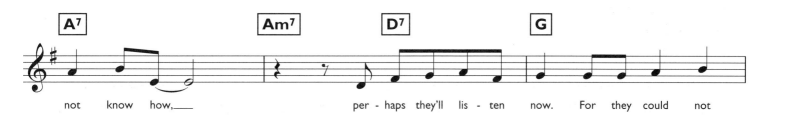

san - i - ty, how you tried to set them free. They would not lis - ten, they did

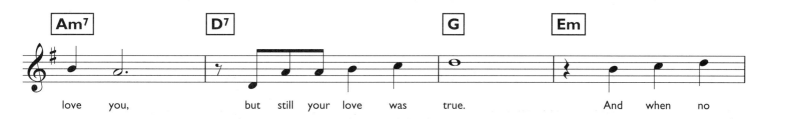

not know how,___ per - haps they'll lis - ten now. For they could not

love you, but still your love was true. And when no

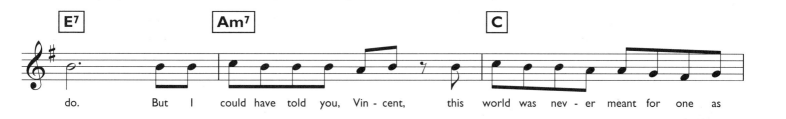

hope was left in sight___ on that star - ry, star - ry night you took your life as lov - ers of - ten

do. But I could have told you, Vin - cent, this world was nev - er meant for one as

beau - ti - ful as you. Star - ry, star - ry night.

Walk On By

Words by Hal David
Music by Burt Bacharach

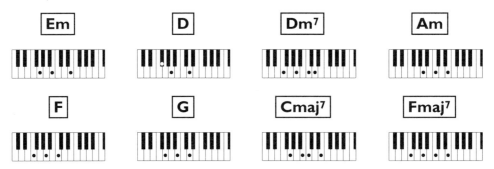

Voice: **Jazz Guitar**
Rhythm: **Bossa Nova**
Tempo: ♩ = 100

If you see me walk - ing down the street, and I start to cry___
I just can't get o - ver los - ing you and if I seem___

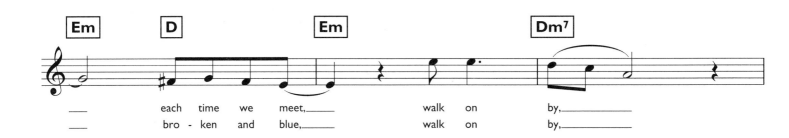

___ each time we meet,___ walk on by,___
___ bro - ken and blue,___ walk on by,___

walk on___ by.___ Make be - lieve___ that
walk on___ by.___ Fool - ish pride___ is

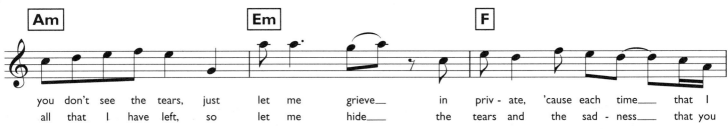

you don't see the tears, just let me grieve___ in priv - ate, 'cause each time___ that I
all that I have left, so let me hide___ the tears and the sad - ness___ that you

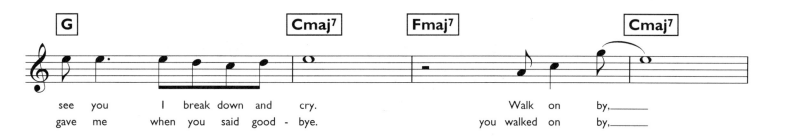

see you   I break down and   cry.   Walk   on   by,_____
gave me   when you said good - bye.   you walked on   by,_____

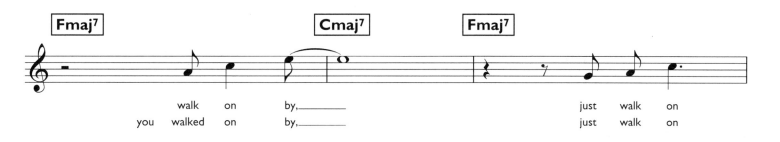

          walk   on   by,_____   just   walk   on
you   walked on   by,_____   just   walk   on

by._____   'Cause   by.

Fool - ish   pride___   is   all that   I have   left,   so   let me   hide___   the

tears and   the sad - ness___   that you   gave me   when you said good - bye.   Walk on   by,__

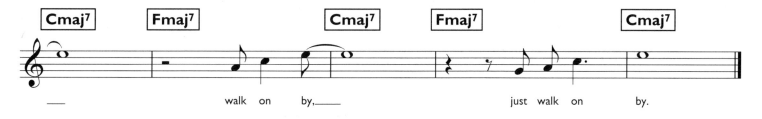

___   gave me   walk on   by,___   just walk on   by.

83

What A Wonderful World

Words & Music by George Weiss & Bob Thiele

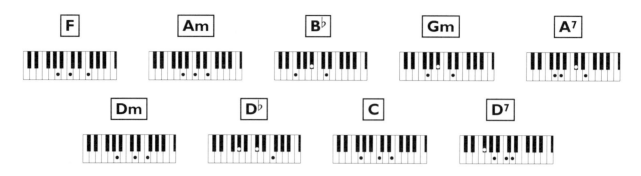

Voice: **Strings**
Rhythm: **Ballad (Triplets)**
Tempo: ♩ =74

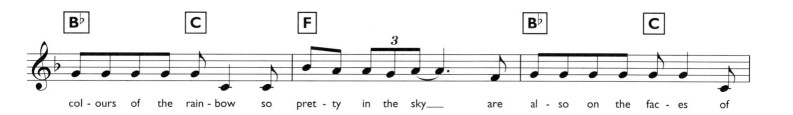

col - ours of the rain - bow so pret - ty in the sky___ are al - so on the fac - es of

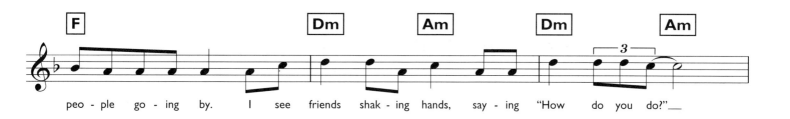

peo - ple go - ing by. I see friends shak - ing hands, say - ing "How do you do?"___

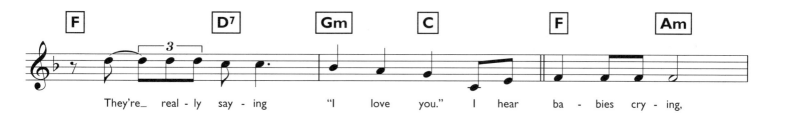

They're_ real - ly say - ing "I love you." I hear ba - bies cry - ing,

I watch them grow. They'll learn much more than I'll ev - er know. And I

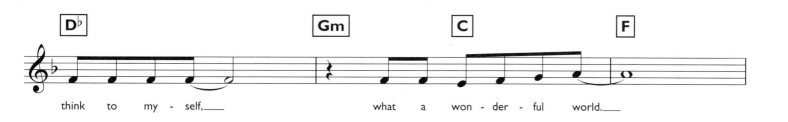

think to my - self,___ what a won - der - ful world.___

Yes I think to my - self,___ what a won - der - ful world.

Wichita Lineman

Words & Music by Jimmy Webb

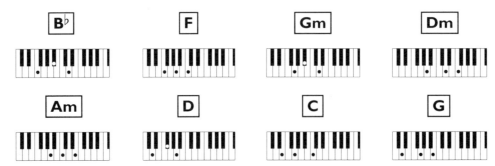

Voice: **Acoustic Guitar**
Rhythm: **Country**
Tempo: ♩ = 88

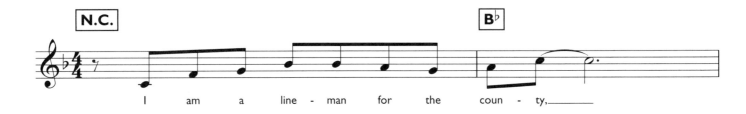

I am a line-man for the coun-ty,

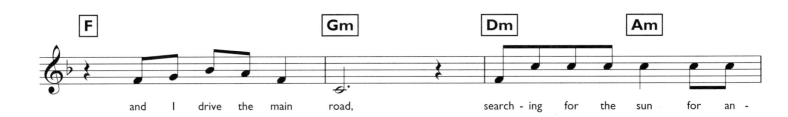

and I drive the main road, search-ing for the sun for an -

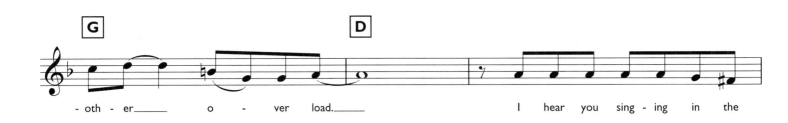

- oth - er___ o - ver load.___ I hear you sing - ing in the

wi - res, I can hear you through the whine,___

and the Wi - chi - ta Line - man is still on the

line._____ I know I need a small va -

- ca - tion, but it don't look like rain. And if it snows, that stretch down south will

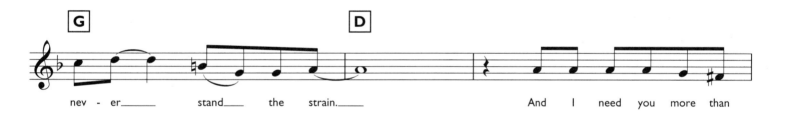

nev - er_____ stand__ the strain.____ And I need you more than

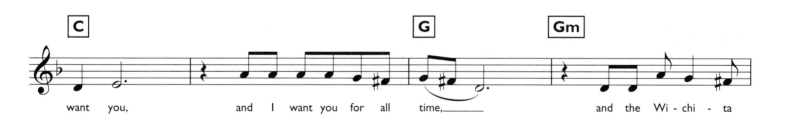

want you, and I want you for all time,_____ and the Wi - chi - ta

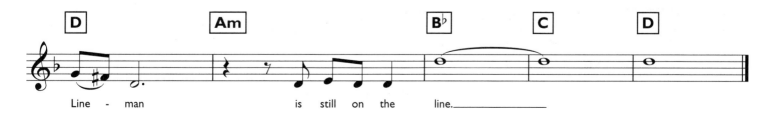

Line - man is still on the line._____

Wondrous Place

Words & Music by Bill Giant & Jeff Lewis

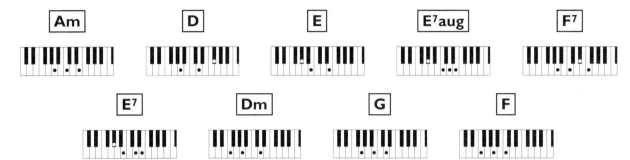

Voice: Flute
Rhythm: Rhumba
Tempo: ♩ = 112

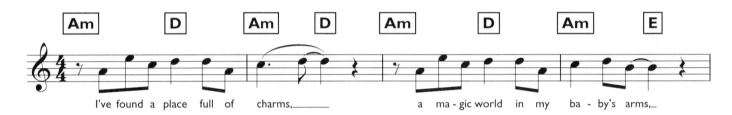

I've found a place full of charms,_____ a ma-gic world in my ba-by's arms,_

her soft em-brace like sa-tin and lace.___ A won-drous place._

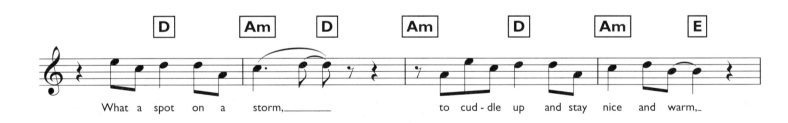

What a spot on a storm,_____ to cud-dle up and stay nice and warm,_

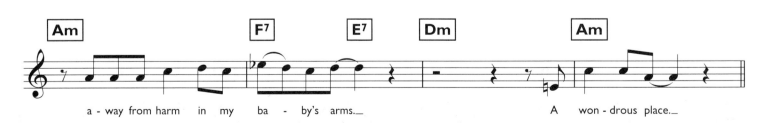

a-way from harm in my ba-by's arms.___ A won-drous place._

Man, I'm____ no - where when I'm an - y - where else.____

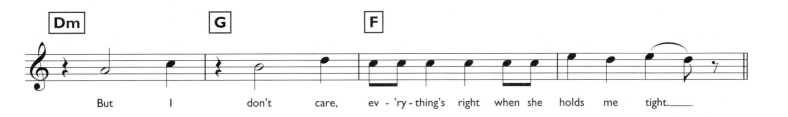

But I don't care, ev - 'ry - thing's right when she holds me tight.____

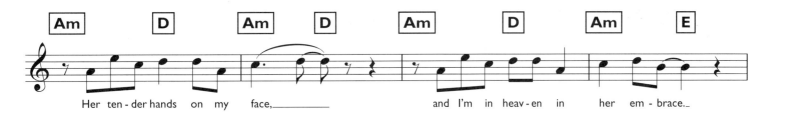

Her ten - der hands on my face,____ and I'm in heav - en in her em - brace.__

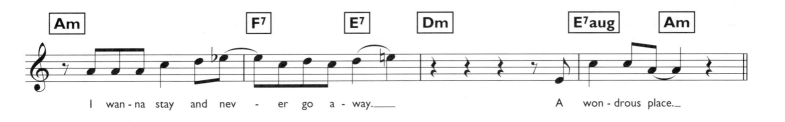

I wan - na stay and nev - er go a - way.____ A won - drous place.__

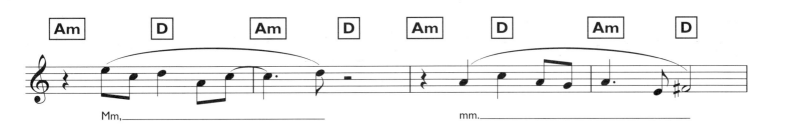

Mm,_____ mm._____

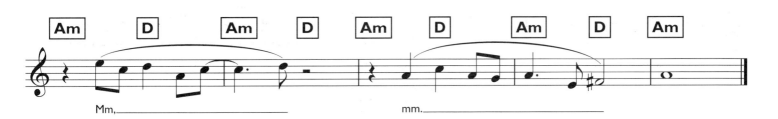

Mm,_____ mm._____

Yesterday Once More

Words & Music by Richard Carpenter & John Bettis

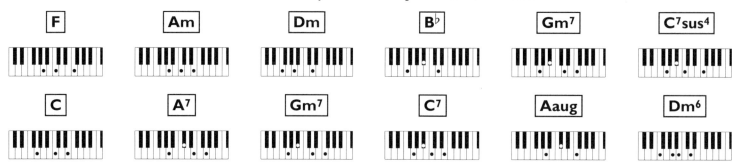

Voice: **Electric piano**
Rhythm: **Bossa Nova**
Tempo: ♩ = 112

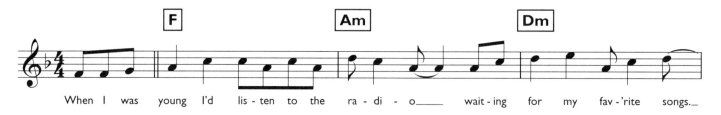

When I was young I'd lis-ten to the ra-di-o___ wait-ing for my fav-'rite songs.___

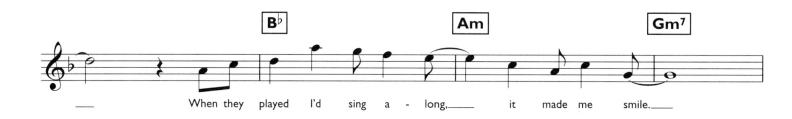

___ When they played I'd sing a-long,___ it made me smile.___

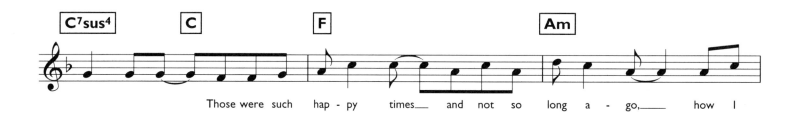

Those were such hap-py times___ and not so long a-go,___ how I

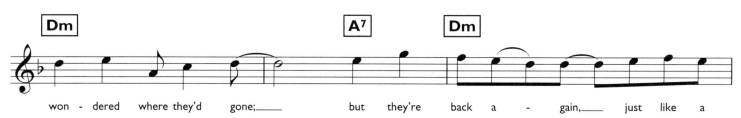

won-dered where they'd gone;___ but they're back a-gain,___ just like a

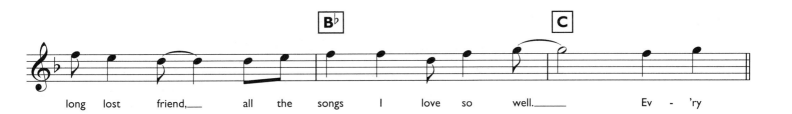

long lost friend,___ all the songs I love so well.___ Ev - 'ry

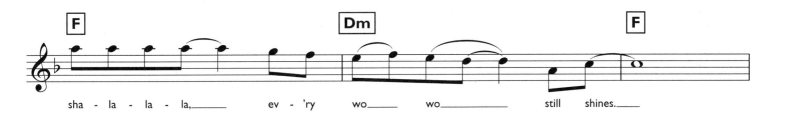

sha - la - la - la,___ ev - 'ry wo___ wo___ still shines.___

Ev - 'ry shing a - ling a - ling that they're start - ing to sing___ so fine.___

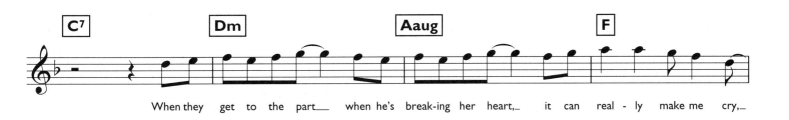

When they get to the part___ when he's break - ing her heart,___ it can real - ly make me cry,___

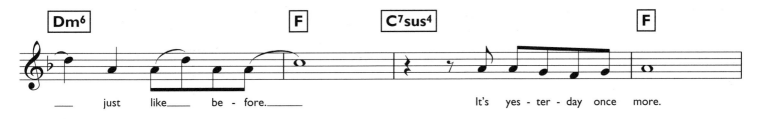

___ just like___ be - fore.___ It's yes - ter - day once more.

Ev - 'ry sha - la - la - la,___ ev - 'ry wo__ wo___ still shines.___

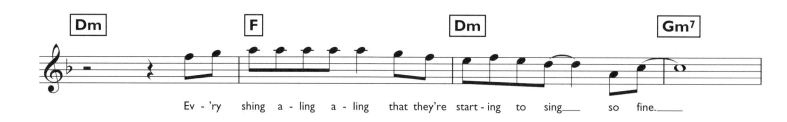

Ev - 'ry shing a - ling a - ling that they're start - ing to sing__ so fine.___

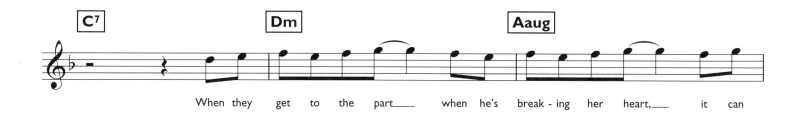

When they get to the part___ when he's break - ing her heart,___ it can

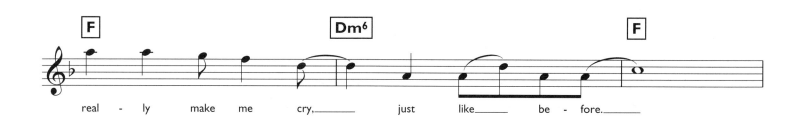

real - ly make me cry,___ just like__ be - fore.___

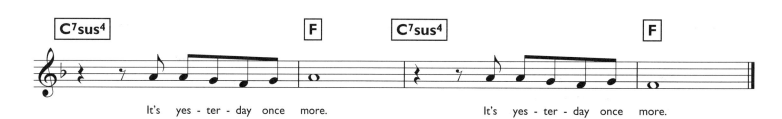

It's yes - ter - day once more.   It's yes - ter - day once more.

You Don't Have To Say You Love Me

Words by Vito Pallavicini
Music by Pino Donaggio
English Words by Vicki Wickham & Simon Napier-Bell

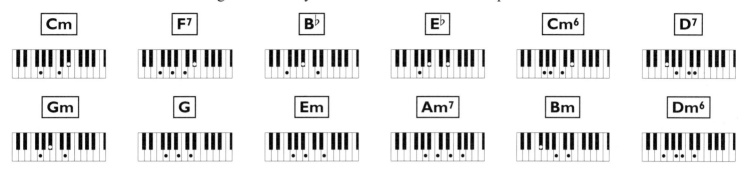

Voice: **Harmonica**
Rhythm: **Swing**
Tempo: ♩ = 84

When I said I need-ed you,_____ you said you would al - ways stay,_____

____ it was-n't me who changed but you, and now you've gone a - way.

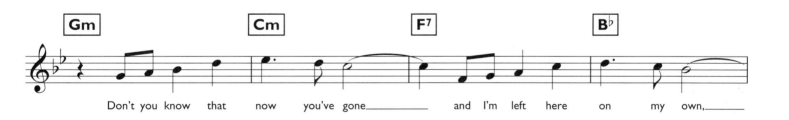

Don't you know that now you've gone_____ and I'm left here on my own,_____

____ now I have to fol - low you and beg you to come home.

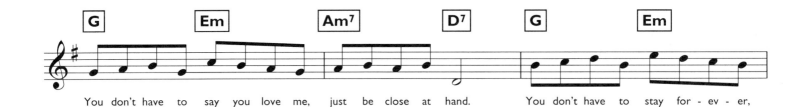

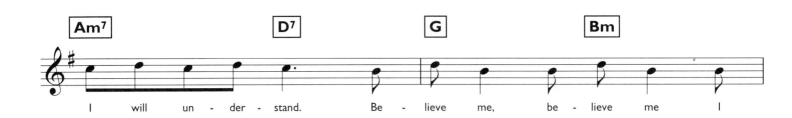

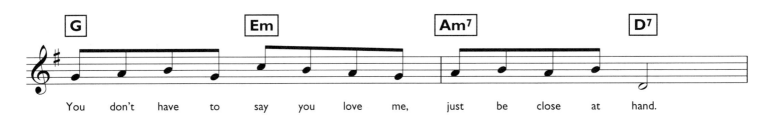

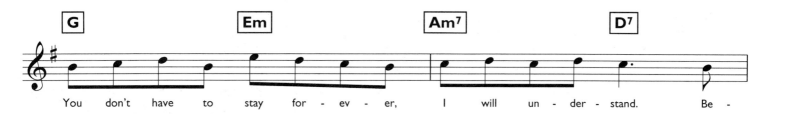

You don't have to stay for - ev - er, I will un - der - stand. Be -

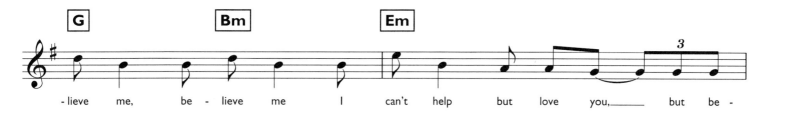

- lieve me, be - lieve me I can't help but love you,_____ but be -

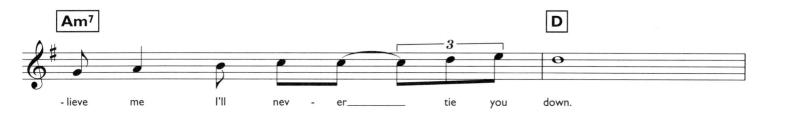

- lieve me I'll nev - er_____ tie you down.

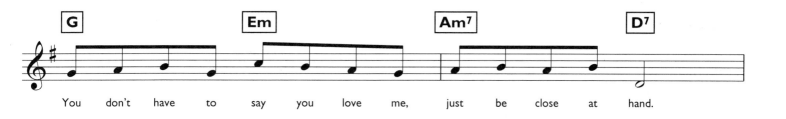

You don't have to say you love me, just be close at hand.

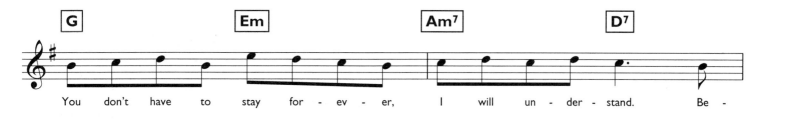

You don't have to stay for - ev - er, I will un - der - stand. Be -

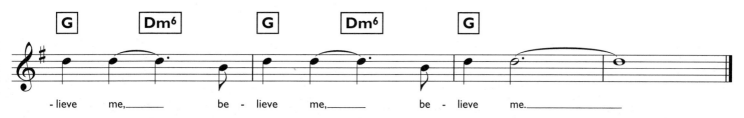

- lieve me,_____ be - lieve me,_____ be - lieve me._____

1 2 3 4 5 6 7 8 9